W9-ADZ-272

HOW TO RAISE A READER

HOW TO RAISE A READER

Elaine K. McEwan

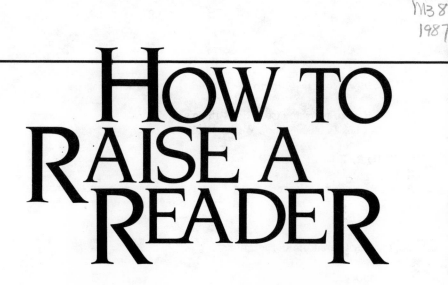

LIFEJOURNEY
BOOKS

LifeJourney Books is an imprint of David C. Cook Publishing Co.

David C. Cook Publishing Co., Elgin, Illinois 60120
David C. Cook Publishing Co., Weston, Ontario

HOW TO RAISE A READER

Designed by GraphCom Corporation

First Printing, 1987
Printed in the United States of America
92 91 90 89 88 87 5 4 3 2 1

Library of Congress Cataloging-in-Publication Data
McEwan, Elaine K.
    How to riase a reader.
    Bibliography: p. 172
    Includes index.
    1. Children—Books and reading.
    2. Reading—Parent participation. I. Title.
Z1037.A1M38   1987   649'.58   87-3973

ISBN 1-55513-211-1

For my children, Emily and Patrick

Contents

Foreword

It was two or three years ago—I can't remember which—
that she came to me, crawled upon my lap dragging behind
her a dog-eared book of pages smeared with magic words and
peanut butter, and suggested (she didn't implore or beg or
demand, but she suggested), "Help me read it, Daddy; help
me read it."

So we talked of such things as talking bears and slow-
witted park rangers; of little blonde girls who get tired, hungry, and sleepy; and of lions that die and live again.

She is gone now; married with a child of her own, so she
doesn't come anymore to sit on my lap. But she does call on
the telephone and suggests, "Help me read it, Daddy. Help
me read it." So we talk of such things as boys growing up
along the banks of the Mississippi; of women who wear letters around their necks; of Aristotelian ethics; and of lions
that die and live again.

This is more than reading—this thing that we have
together—she and I—it is memories and the kind of relationship you can build your life around.

My friend, Elaine, has written this book about reading.
She has a right to do that. She is an expert, a professional.
For years, she has taught others how to read, and she has
taught others how to teach others how to read. Experience
and training make her an expert. Oh, some other expert

might disagree with some of what she says. Experts do that, you know. If experts never disagreed, there would be no need for conventions, and all the hotels would go broke.

But read carefully. Elaine knows what she is talking about. Her ideas work. Hundreds of readers prove that.

But Elaine has written more than a book about reading. She has written about memories and the kind of relationship you can build your life around. She has a right to do that. She is a mother, and her ideas put into practice will do more than teach your child to read. They will teach you to love and care as well.

I envy you a bit—those of you who want to read this book, who need to read this book. I envy you for the memories that lie ahead. But I warn you, too. Be aware! Those three years between birth and adulthood pass quickly—when you look back.

So read this book. Keep it on the nightstand beside your bed so that you can plan ahead or check back. But the book alone won't do the job, can't do the job. Find the time; make the time to build a reader—and some memories—and the kind of relationship you can build a life around.

> Cliff Schimmels
> teacher, pastor,
> principal, parent

Introduction

You are about to embark on one of the most exciting adventures that awaits any parent. The Scriptures challenge us to raise our children in the ways of the Lord so that when they are grown they will continue in these ways. The ways of reading are inextricably linked to the ways of God. The Christian must be able to read in order to nourish his faith in God's Holy Word. Therefore the Biblical charge to raise a child in the ways of God carries with it a responsibility to raise a child who can read.

The day I stepped into an elementary classroom fresh from Wheaton College, I began structuring my classes around my own love for books and the great joy that reading brought to my life. I read aloud regularly to my students and encouraged them to read during every spare moment. We talked about the books. We drew posters and made mobiles to illustrate our books. We even dressed up in costume as our favorite historical figures after reading biographies.

But I wasn't satisfied at having an impact on only one classroom of children. I went back to school and became a library learning center teacher. As a librarian, I could motivate and inspire all age levels to read and interact with books. I could motivate teachers to read to their classes and have story hours regularly for everyone. Then I interrupted my teaching career to raise a family.

As the mother of two children, I began to investigate the learning capabilities of infants and toddlers. I began to test some of the theories I had developed in working with children during my years as an educator. Now I had to live with my mistakes. I couldn't use the time-honored phrase I had sometimes used in reference to a particularly difficult student: "Just look at his home environment." I learned my best lessons about children and reading while working with Emily and Patrick, my children.

I learned that the lessons we yearn for our children to learn about God, the Christian world view, and how we deal with life as Christians could be taught through reading aloud. Words that flow from the pen of a skilled author can sometimes say in a much more effective way that which we would like to say to our children. The words we read aloud to our children can be our personal testimony to them about what we believe and value.

When my children were launched into elementary school, I returned to the world of school libraries; once again I felt the need to reach more children. I went back to school and earned another degree, a doctorate in educational administration. As an elementary school principal I began to see in a more immediate way the devastation that parents and students experience when school is difficult and reading does not come easily.

I encouraged parents to work with their children at home, developed reading incentive and tutoring programs, and worked with teachers to improve reading instruction in our school. All of these endeavors produced results: our reading scores went up. All children can learn to read, but I knew that we could do so much more if our students came to us with a love for books and reading that had started at birth. I began to wonder what I could do to spread the word to even more parents about the importance of reading in the lives of their children. The result—*How to Raise a Reader*.

You can read this book in a variety of ways. Chapters one

and two are organized in a question and answer format. Just flip through them to find what you want to know.

Chapters three, four, and five describe children of different ages and give suggestions for books to read aloud that are appropriate for them—from infancy to age ten. If you are already well on your way to raising a reader, you may only need some good ideas for read alouds. Use these chapters as a resource. Chapter six gives you a list of books to entice the reluctant reader to do more independent reading.

If your child already attends school, chapter seven provides some strategies for evaluating your school on its RQ (Reading Quotient). It goes on to give you practical suggestions for becoming involved to improve your school's RQ.

If your child is having problems with reading, chapter eight gives some suggestions for working with him to improve reading performance.

Finally, chapter nine warns of some common mistakes we parents sometimes make in our zeal to raise readers and discusses ways to avoid these errors.

I pray that you will find answers to your questions about how to reach your goal of raising a child who can read in the chapters ahead.

1

"I Learned To Read Today"

When my first child went off to kindergarten, I experienced all of the usual emotions. Not only was she leaving the nest, but in those new surroundings she would be instructed, examined, and evaluated. Would she measure up? Would she have fun? Would she like school? And, most important to me, would she learn to read? I already knew my daughter Emily liked books. She was always ready to sit down and listen to a story, and frequently she asked for a story to be read aloud.

I also knew that she understood and remembered almost everything we read together. But I had no idea if she could or even would learn to read. My earlier attempts at teaching her had not been notable. I had purchased a "miracle" toilet training book that promised success in less than a day. The book had not accounted for Emily's stubborn nature. The book promised pride and a sense of accomplishment for the child and parent. I must have been one of their few failures if the book jacket was to be believed. Consequently I didn't even attempt to teach her to read. I decided the joyful experience we shared together with books was too special to turn it into a battleground.

She went off to kindergarten with anticipation. She was not disappointed. One day, about a month into the school year, Emily arrived home and announced, "I learned to read today." I couldn't believe what I was hearing. Perhaps she had confused writing letters on a paper with reading. "Can you read for me?" I asked her with barely contained excitement.

"Oh, no," she stated emphatically. "Reading is something you only do at school. I can't do it for you at home." Now my curiosity was overwhelming. I pulled several "I Can Read" books off the shelves and used my best child psychology methods on her. (The same ones that had worked so successfully with toilet training.)

"I'll buy you an ice cream cone at The Plush Horse if you'll read something for me."

"I'm hungry for lunch. I told you—you only read at school." She was firm in her resolve.

Clearly my methods would have to be more clever in order to get a demonstration of this newly learned skill. Bribery was too obvious. For the next few days I kept asking her to read words on cereal boxes or billboards for me. She refused.

Finally when she could take my harassment no longer, she consented. "All right," she agreed grudgingly. "But I can't do it for very long. You're only supposed to read in school." Eagerly I pulled out the same "I Can Read" books. She promptly sat down and began reading aloud to me with fluency and expression as if this were something we had been doing regularly.

In actuality, reading aloud was something we had been doing regularly. Only now the roles were reversed. My child was reading to me. At that moment I realized that in her mind, she had learned to read in one day at school. She was not yet aware that the preparation for this moment when she was actually reading had been going on since she was a baby. The preparation for this moment had been five years of continuing conversation, incessant questions, endless repetitions of nursery rhymes and poems, and the reading aloud of hundreds of her favorite picture books.

However, the question is not *when* your child learns to

read, but the ease with which he is able to learn because of the rich experiences you have given him by reading aloud.

A story about my second child Patrick illustrates that point. He loved kindergarten and received the highest praise from his teacher. But there were no signs that he was a fluent reader. He knew his alphabet and dutifully completed the worksheets of our kindergarten reading program. But he never sat down to read aloud to me as his sister had done. He entered first grade and did very well with the traditional first grade curriculum. We continued to read aloud every night—books he brought home from the school library, books from the public library, and the old favorites from preschool. He read to me from the simple first grade readers. He was learning to read in the more traditional way—*but* he was experiencing success every step of the way.

In second grade, he discovered the joy of reading and truly began to read. His teacher, one he still reveres, had a reading incentive program. Patrick read over 1000 books during that year and by April was reading full-length novels like *Charlotte's Web* and *Ramona and Her Father*.

In the pages ahead, you will find answers to many questions you, as a Christian, have had about your child and reading. All parents want their children to enjoy the benefits of being a good reader. But more importantly, all Christian parents desire a personal salvation and knowledge of God's will for their children. Only through reading God's Word and learning the lessons taught in its pages can our children come to know Him.

WHAT IS READING?

Some people think that once a child has pronounced a word, either silently or orally, she is reading. But pronouncing the word is only word identification. Of course that's a basic prerequisite to reading. But word identification is not reading. It's *word calling*. What a child needs in order to be reading is meaning or comprehension. The child needs to understand, react, and learn from the printed page in order to be reading.

I frequently visit in classrooms where Hispanic students are beginning to read English for the first time. I can listen to them "read" aloud and make the assumption that they are reading. However, I know by their blank stares when I ask them questions about what they've read that they are not *really* reading. They understand the rules for pronouncing words in English, but only when they master all the new vocabulary and understand what it means will they truly be reading English.

The best formal definition of reading says: "Reading is the meaningful interpretation of printed or written verbal symbols."[1]

The key words in this definition are *meaningful interpretation*. For reading to take place, the reader must gain meaning.

WHY IS READING SO IMPORTANT?

I asked a group of kindergarten parents at orientation what they wanted their children to learn at school this year. The majority answered, "To learn how to read." Success in any school system is based on reading ability. A child's self concept of himself as a student is frequently based on his earliest experiences with learning to read. Our testing programs are based on the ability to read. But most importantly, reading is our link with the world. It lets us share ideas, travel, learn, experience the pain and joys of others, and enrich our lives.

Illiteracy is one of our country's biggest social problems. The U.S. Department of Education estimates that twenty-seven million Americans can't decipher a street sign or the number on a bus, and forty-five million have never read a book or newspaper. These people are cut off from the things you and I take for granted. More importantly, they are unable to function effectively in our society.

HOW DO CHILDREN LEARN TO READ?

Thousands of volumes have been written on the teaching of reading. Professors and teachers by the score have learned how to teach reading. Or at least they think they have. Stop for a moment of reflection on how many courses are offered on the teaching of talking. We don't *teach* our children how to talk. We *talk* to them. They learn to read in the very same way—when we *read* to them. A child can only learn to talk by talking. That same child can only learn to read by reading.

What happens when a small child utters an incomprehensible phrase? We attempt to understand what was said and restate what we thought was said. We engage in conversation. We give feedback to the child. Meanwhile, the child is constantly figuring out the rules for this "talking game" and trying out new variations all the time. By three years of age, the child who has been engaged in constant face-to-face interaction and communication with caring adults understands most of the language that he will use in ordinary conversation for the rest of his life.[2]

The same patterns hold true for the printed word as for the spoken word. If a child hears the printed word read aloud from birth, she will develop a curiosity to figure out the rules for reading just as she figured out the rules for talking. Children begin learning to read when adults make sense out of the printed page for them. They learn something more about reading every time we read aloud to them.

Children learn that individual letters have different names, that certain letters make certain sounds, and that combinations of letters stand for words. They read their name, the street signs, simple words like *ball* and *cat* and soon they are deciphering all kinds of words and bringing meaning to the printed page. Adults can learn to read in the very same way once they overcome the self-doubts and failure that accompanied their first attempts at learning to read.

WHAT ARE THE MOST IMPORTANT THINGS I CAN DO TO HELP MY CHILD LEARN TO READ?

Please take note: This question does not say "How can I *teach* my child to read?" We are making it possible for our children to *learn* to read. We are not *teaching* them to read.

Researchers have always been fascinated by children who came to school already knowing how to read. Some teachers were delighted. Some were annoyed. "That's our job," they said. "Parents should leave the teaching of reading to the professionals." What many teachers didn't realize, as in the case with my daughter, was that we didn't deliberately teach them—they learned on their own.

What was happening in the homes of these children that was different from what was taking place in other homes? Researchers interviewed parents to discover the common elements.[3] There were four:

1. Reading took place in the home. Parents read to children regularly. They themselves read. Reading was a part of the family life-style.

2. A wide range of printed materials was available in the home. Magazines, books of all kinds, and newspapers were part of the interior decorating scheme.

3. Children had lots of contact with paper and pencil. (Perhaps in this modern age, our learners will have contact with computer terminals and word processors.) Children were able to produce their own scribbles and scrawls and do their own "writing."

4. Finally, all of the adults in the environment responded to what the child was trying to do. They took very seriously his attempts to make sense out of the written and spoken word.

Let me explain this last statement with an example. Sally is a highly organized and efficient mother. She makes

Christmas ornaments in her family room and sells them at craft shows. Her toddler, Adam, plays nearby while she works. Adam frequently interrupts her work to comment or ask a question. Whenever he does, Sally tunes in. She answers as though she were conversing with a close friend. Overhearing her conversation you might even suspect she was talking to an adult. There is no "baby talk." She is not condescending. Sally could very well say, "Don't interrupt me. Can't you see I'm working?" She could nod absently and say, "That's nice, honey." Or, in the worst of all possible scenarios, she could totally ignore the childish chatter. But she thinks talking to her toddler is one of the most important things she can do. She is absolutely right.

WHAT IF THERE ISN'T ENOUGH TIME TO READ ALOUD TO MY CHILD?

The kindergarten teacher in my elementary school has developed a very effective technique to encourage those parents who think they don't have time to read aloud to their children. The technique is somewhat similar to the way in which commercials persuade you to buy those wonderful, sugar-coated cereals. She works through her students.

The children fill out slips for each book their parents read aloud to them. When they turn in the slips to their teacher, they receive stars on a chart. When the children have a certain number of stars, they receive a certificate. Soon the children are relentlessly hounding their parents to read aloud. The parents give in just to get peace.

I hope I can convince you that you must find the time to read to your child. We know it's almost as important a part of your child's daily routine as brushing his teeth. I have laughingly joked with parents that we have all the technology necessary to repair teeth. Repairing reading problems is a far more complex task.

We do have the time—we just don't use it. How about the

waiting room at the doctor's office? How about while you're waiting for that long freight train? How about when you're dying to put your feet up and relax and the kids won't leave you alone? Whenever you've run out of entertainment ideas, try a book. One of our favorite times was just before bed. I could almost feel the stress and tension leave our bodies and minds as we quietly read aloud one of our favorites like *Good Night Moon* or *Bedtime for Frances*. Reading aloud is a wonderful transition between an active, busy day and your child's willing trip up the stairs to bed.

SHOULDN'T READING INSTRUCTION BE LEFT TO TRAINED TEACHERS IN THE SCHOOLS?

You can leave *formal* reading instruction to the schools. But think of all of the shared experiences, background, and knowledge your child will bring to formal instruction if you begin reading aloud in infancy. We never can go back to those precious years with their enormous potential for learning once they are gone.

Dr. Burton J. White, a respected physician and researcher at Harvard University in the field of child development, has said, "Relatively few families, perhaps no more than ten percent, manage to get their children through the eight to thirty-six month age period as well educated and developed as they can and should be."[4] Dr. White is not talking about enrolling your child in lessons and courses. He is not talking about hiring specialists to teach your child. He is talking about being aware of the enormous potential for informal learning that exists in the home through parent-child interaction.

You don't need degrees and diplomas. You don't need the trappings of technology. You don't need to be remarkably learned about education and psychology. You only need a remarkable respect for the mind of a child, a willingness to be consistent, and lots of patience.

WHAT ELSE CAN BE DONE IN ADDITION TO READING ALOUD IN ORDER TO RAISE A READER?

Many of the things you can do in addition to reading aloud have already been noted, but they are worth mentioning again in the following checklist. Use it to test your commitment to raising a reader.

☐ Do I help my children seek their own solutions to problems?

☐ Am I open-minded and receptive to my children's ideas?

☐ Do I have places in my home for relaxing and reading both for children and adults?

☐ Do I have a family bulletin board or place for the children's projects and written work to be displayed? (The refrigerator with colorful magnets is an ideal spot.)

☐ Do my children have a special place where they can store their own books to read whenever they want?

☐ Do I talk to my children about my work and explain what I am doing and why? (The kitchen or workshop are wonderful places to talk.)

☐ Do I provide experiences for my children that are reading related—such as library story hours, listening to read-aloud cassettes and records?

☐ Do I provide writing materials and give my children an opportunity to create their own stories? (They may have to explain them to you since the scribbles will frequently be unintelligible to an adult.) An old typewriter provided a place for Emily to "write books." She filled pages with random letters, drew illustrations, and told her stories to me.

☐ Do I capture every opportunity for reading as we take trips and run errands together—such as reading street signs, grocery store displays, and other types of informational signs?

☐ Do I know what my children's interests are and do I

capitalize on those interests to stimulate reading—such as zoo animals, trucks, dinosaurs?

☐ Do I buy books as well as borrow them from the library?

☐ Do I use the developmental stages that my children are in to teach appropriate lessons through reading—such as need for sharing, being kind to others?

☐ Do I use the printed materials that come home from Sunday school as read-aloud materials during the week?

☐ Am I sensitive to the curious nature of my child's mind and heart regarding spiritual matters, and do I use the read-aloud experience to help answer these questions? (Where is heaven? Why do people die? Can God see everything I do?)

☐ Do I choose to read books, including God's Word, and make printed materials a part of my own home?

WON'T MY CHILD HAVE PROBLEMS IN SCHOOL IF HE ALREADY KNOWS HOW TO READ?

The child who enters school already knowing how to read will have much smoother sailing than the child who has reading problems. In either case, parents must be ready to intervene and work *with* the school. Enrichment programs, learning center activities, peer tutoring, or accelerated placement are all possible solutions for the child who is ahead of his age-mates.

CAN A PARENT WHO IS A POOR READER OR DOESN'T LIKE TO READ RAISE A READER?

ABSOLUTELY! Many of the parents I have worked with have found that once they began reading aloud to their children, they gained confidence and skills in their own reading abilities. They just hadn't practiced enough. Your preschooler is a very uncritical audience.

Maybe the reasons you don't like to read will wash away as you discover the joy that comes in sharing books with your child. Discipline yourself in the beginning. I predict you'll be hooked on reading yourself before very long. Some of the best children's literature can absolutely delight an adult. Try it!

ISN'T READING ALOUD JUST ANOTHER RECIPE FOR PUSHING KIDS TOO FAST AND NOT ALLOWING THEM TO GROW UP NATURALLY?

I am sensitive to the recent trend by upwardly mobile parents to raise "superkids." Reading aloud to children is the reverse of that trend. Reading aloud takes time, patience, involves one-to-one parent-child interaction, and requires a sensitivity to the needs and interests of the individual child. It is quiet. It is unhurried. The rewards are definitely long term, and there are many detours and side streets before you reach your destination.

The rewards of raising a reader are subtle. Your child will seldom be bored. Your child will have interesting ideas and value your opinions. Your child will never stop learning.

2

"Read It One More Time, Daddy"

My husband was raised in the city. I was raised in the country. His family always planted a garden on their thirty-foot lot. My family bought all of its produce at my father's grocery store. My husband's family took summer vacations in different places. We always stayed at home because Dad had to tend to the store. Despite our many differences, we did find a common thread running through our childhoods—the importance of reading in our families.

There were always books, newspapers, and magazines strewn about the house in spite of my mother's fanatical attention to housekeeping and cleanliness. My mother read new Sunday school curriculum materials and *Moody Monthly* while my father read business magazines, trade journals, and newspapers. In my husband's family, reading tastes ran to poetry and classics. But our families did agree that reading was important.

I have memories of my mother reading aloud to comfort and quiet me when I had the measles, memories of bicycling over two miles each week to the bookmobile that visited our rural area, and memories of gliding back and forth on the porch swing while curled up with a book. My husband remembers his father telling folktales and adventure stories of the sea; he remembers making the difficult decision about which fourteen books he would choose from the public library to take along on his summer vacation. And he remembers swinging on a porch swing similar to mine while reading a favorite adventure story.

When we talked about becoming parents we always mentioned creating those same warm feelings and good memories about books and reading for our children. We began to purchase children's books even before we had children.

If you have a desire to raise a reader as we did and have questions about how to begin, this chapter will help you. You will find out why reading aloud is one of the most important shared experiences you can have with your children, when and how you should begin reading aloud, and how to choose appropriate materials to read aloud.

WHAT IS READING ALOUD?

Perhaps you're wondering why we even need to define reading aloud. But the dismal statistics regarding illiteracy, drop out rates, and enrollments in remedial reading classes show that for many people, reading aloud must have been an uncommon experience.

Reading aloud is a shared experience in which one person reads a story or entire book to another person or group. Reading aloud takes place in church each Sunday as the minister reads the Scripture to his congregation. Reading aloud takes place each time a parent puts a child on his lap and makes a story come to life.

WHAT ARE THE BENEFITS OF READING ALOUD?

Books have a marvelous capacity for helping adults to build relationships with children. Reading a book together gives adult and child a shared background and experience. When my children and I see a spider building a web in the corner of a room, we immediately think of Charlotte, that famous spider from E.B. White's classic, *Charlotte's Web*.

When we have breaded veal cutlets for dinner, our family shares a moment of fun singing Frances's song about what veal cutlets wear before they're breaded from the delightful story, *Bread and Jam for Frances*.

Reading aloud gives the child an understanding of the purpose of the printed word and a growing familiarity with written language that is essential to a successful experience with reading in school.

My sixteen-year-old daughter Emily had just started driver's training. Getting her ready to drive a car had not been high on our list of priorities during the year. Her father felt that he didn't have the patience. I felt I didn't have the time. Therefore she entered the class with no background, no hands-on experience, and no support from home.

She came home after the first class and said her teacher was astounded that she had never driven a car before. "How did you reach the age of sixteen without ever starting a car or experimenting with backing out of the driveway?" he asked. Other members of her driving group already knew how to drive. The class was only giving them the credential they needed and fine tuning any problems.

This experience tells me that many parents are not willing to entrust driver's education to the schools. They want to be involved. I wonder if these same parents had an equal concern for their child's readiness to learn reading skills before he started kindergarten.

Just suppose that this experience had been my daughter's first time in a classroom. Suppose she was behind before she even started with other members of her class because of their prior experiences and home environments. Just suppose that her feelings about herself as a person and learner were going to be shaped forever by this obvious deficiency on her part. How would she then feel about driving? How would she begin to feel about herself as a person?

Instead of a confident sixteen year old, change the student to a fearful five year old. She is starting school with classmates who have been exposed to books since birth. They know about the connection between the spoken and written word. They know about how much you can learn from books. They know how to sit and listen. They've already absorbed vast amounts of information about the world and how it works from listening to stories being read aloud. Indeed, they may already know how to read.

Young children have an enormous capacity for learning. Reading a wide variety of books will give them a chance to learn about human emotions, other kinds of people and places, Bible stories, trucks, trains, animals, plants, and famous people. The list is endless.

For many parents there are two important reasons for reading aloud. You'll have fun while developing a closer relationship with your child. And your child will grow up to be a reader.

But for the Christian parent, the reasons for reading aloud are even more compelling. We have been challenged in the Scriptures to raise our children in the ways of the Lord. In order to nourish his faith in God's Holy Word, the Christian must be able to read. Therefore the Biblical charge to raise a child in the ways of God carries with it a responsibility to raise a child who can read.

WHO SHOULD READ ALOUD?

Is reading aloud so difficult and important that only specially trained people can do it? Of course not. Everyone who cares for the child should read aloud regularly.

The summer my children were three and five, I worked as the librarian for a remedial reading project. My children needed care while I was away. I interviewed a number of high school students and finally selected Joan, an energetic young woman with excellent references. I was only gone for about three hours each day, but I helped her put together a schedule that would keep the children busy and happy. A little water play in the wading pool, a walk to the local park, a snack on the patio, riding Big Wheels on the driveway, and of course reading aloud several stories.

When I returned from work each day, I talked with the children to find out what they had been doing. One part of the schedule never seemed to be completed—the reading of stories. I mentioned it to Joan on more than one occasion. She always smiled and nodded. But somehow the stories never got read. Although she followed all of my other instructions to the letter, I soon realized that Joan wasn't going to read the stories. I didn't pressure her. Perhaps she had some reading problems. I didn't want to embarrass her in front of the children.

The summer job was soon over. I didn't ask Joan to return as a sitter. I wanted anyone who spent time with my children to enjoy reading and to spend time reading aloud to them.

Fathers should most definitely read to their children. All of the shared experiences shouldn't just be Mom's and the kids'. My favorite snapshot shows my husband snuggled up in our big leather chair reading *Davy and His Dog* to a freshly bathed and ready-for-bed fourteen month old. She is pointing to the dog, and her father looks absolutely entranced by this delightful experience.

Older brothers and sisters can read to younger children also. Grandparents and aunts and uncles can be enlisted as well. Baby-sitters should read aloud. And of course, teachers should read aloud.

WHEN SHOULD I BEGIN READING ALOUD?

The minute I found out we were expecting our first child, I started reading books about pregnancy, child care, and child development. I read everything our public library had available. One book in particular made sense to me. It was called *How to Raise a Brighter Child*.[1] Some of the ideas were new. Some were controversial. Researchers were just beginning to find out that the period from birth to three years was crucial in terms of development. The book emphasized the importance of treating your infant as a person from the very beginning, talking to her and reading to her.

When Emily wouldn't sleep in the middle of the night, I held her in the rocking chair while reciting poems and nursery rhymes, singing songs, and telling her Bible stories. Those story-telling sessions got me through many sleepless nights. When she was about six months of age, I began reading to her from easy books. I talked to her all the time. In the beginning I felt a little foolish conversing with an infant. Sometimes people would look at me strangely in the grocery store while I carried on a seemingly one-sided conversation with an immobile baby. But I chattered on.

Recite poems, rhymes, and songs from the very beginning. Start reading simple stories to your baby at about six months of age. Don't make the mistake of thinking that because your baby isn't responding in some way that he is not learning.

WHERE SHOULD I READ ALOUD?

The wonderful thing about books is their portability. I always carried a couple in the car. The Chicago suburb in which we live is divided into north and south by railroad tracks. Commuter trains roar by several times each hour, with mile-long freight trains stopping lines of traffic at least three times per day. We often read while waiting for the train to go by. Reading aloud has a wonderful way of calming restless children.

I was always grateful to those wonderful doctors and dentists who kept an ample supply of children's books in their waiting rooms so we could fill seemingly endless moments with reading aloud.

You will need to have a comfortable spot designated as

the "read-aloud" spot in your home. Maybe a big, overstuffed chair, if you're reading to just one child, will be the perfect spot. Maybe the heirloom rocking chair in the nursery. When you're reading to two children, you'll need a comfortable couch. Where you read aloud, although all participants should be comfortable, is not nearly as important as the fact that you are doing it.

HOW OFTEN SHOULD I READ ALOUD?

When children are very small, we have to read aloud when they are receptive and ready, not necessarily on our own timetable. But very soon, habits will be formed and they will learn to expect stories every day, as regularly as they expect three meals.

Those who are flexible, easy-going, unplanned, and spontaneous will need to concentrate on making sure that reading aloud occurs with regularity every day. People who are programmed, structured, planned, and organized will need to work on meeting their child's need for flexibility. You should not attempt to read aloud when your child obviously has other needs or interest.

HOW LONG SHOULD I SPEND IN MY READ-ALOUD SESSIONS?

As parents, we must be sensitive to the developmental stages and individual needs of our children. We've all seen hysterical children being dragged through shopping centers during the late evening hours. I know their behavior is not the result of their being "bad" children. Their parents simply haven't been sensitive to their needs for early bedtime or possibly a snack break.

The same principle applies to read-aloud sessions. Capitalize on every quiet moment you can with your active toddler or preschooler. If he is ready for a story and asks for one, be prepared to drop what you're doing and respond. But don't force a child to sit and listen when he is scrambling off your lap. Don't turn the read-aloud time into a battle of wills. Five or six minutes of quiet reading will be the maximum in the beginning. As children's attention spans increase and their interests mature, you can stretch this time. Be prepared, however, for those children who will listen to as many stories at bedtime as you are willing to read.

WHAT SHOULD I READ ALOUD?

I thought you'd never ask. One of the most delightful tasks of parenting is the fun of exploring the wonderful world of children's literature and choosing from among the thousands, those books that you will share with your child.

While preparing to be an elementary teacher I took a course in children's literature at Wheaton College. Dr. Roger Shuy was the teacher, and he did a marvelous job of making children's books come alive. While earning my degree in library science, I took more courses in children's literature.

But reading children's books to fulfill academic requirements is not nearly as rewarding as reading them to real children. Only as books are read aloud do you begin to appreciate what is really appropriate in a read aloud. Choosing children's books is not a science. Selection is a very personal matter; however, chapters three, four, and five will help you. All of the books have been personally field tested for their readability and carefully examined for their age and content recommendations. You will find both Christian and secular books that will make reading aloud to your child a rewarding experience.

But, you have permission to include others in your list of favorites or cross over from one age grouping to another. *These are only recommendations.*

Here are some guidelines for you to use in choosing books. Choose books that you like. If you don't like a story, you will obviously have a difficult time reading it aloud with enthusiasm and enjoyment.

Choose books that interest your child. These interests will become evident as your child grows older. Does she clap with delight whenever you encounter dogs or cats? Why not read *Angus and the Cat* by Marjorie Flack? Is he fascinated by the trains you see each time you go to the grocery store? Check out *The Little Train* by Lois Lenski from the public library. Buy your own copy of that classic *Pat the Bunny* by Dorothy Kunhardt if your preschooler loves to get involved in what she is reading. She can pat the fuzzy bunny, play peek-a-boo, and look in the mirror.

If your child loves rhymes, read aloud from *My Book of Bible Rhymes,* that absolutely marvelous collection of Biblical verse.

You can afford to be less rigid in your selection standards if you are borrowing books from your church or public library, since any mistakes you make in choosing need only be returned next trip. When you begin to purchase books for your child's personal library, make sure that you buy with care. There are many reference books in addition to chapters four, five, and six that can help you make intelligent selections.[2]

WHERE SHOULD I GET THE BOOKS TO READ ALOUD?

Bookstores and libraries are the two major sources for read alouds. When you get your children into the read-aloud habit you will need both. Libraries will give you the variety and quantity you need to keep even the most prolific read-aloud family supplied.

However, the joy a child receives from having his own books is also an important aspect of raising a reader.

Our purchased books came from several sources. Our grocery store had a large section of Golden Books. They were sturdy, colorful, inexpensive, and if chosen with care, were good read alouds. My children were able to help in the selection, and even if we made an occasional mistake, no major investment had been made.

Our favorites from the Christian bookstore were the Arch paperbacks that rhymed the favorite Bible stories—*The Man Caught by a Fish* and *The Braggy King of Babylon*. The Happy Day Books are a wonderful Christian counterpart to the Golden Books mentioned earlier. Chapters three, four, and five contain an abundance of Christian titles that are suitable for reading aloud.

One excellent bookstore was staffed by knowledgeable sales people who were willing to special order and make personal recommendations. I often purchased books there after reading reviews or previewing books at public library.

We always bought hardcover editions of our very favorites, knowing that these would be treasured and read aloud to our children's children. I can foresee the day when we will have a difficult time sorting out which child gets to permanently keep *The Very Hungry Caterpillar* since we only have one copy. It is autographed with a special drawing and signature by the author, Eric Carle. Patrick has already put in his claim for *Robert the Rose Horse*. With her penchant for fantasy, Emily has earmarked the *Chronicles of Narnia* by C.S. Lewis as her own.

Access to a large bookstore gave us the opportunity to purchase best sellers and new editions of children's books. Birthdays and holidays have always been celebrated at our house with gifts of books since my husband passed by a large bookstore on the way to his Chicago office. He frequently purchased a book as a special surprise. In fact, I always knew when he had endured a particularly bad day at the office. He usually left early and browsed in the bookstore to relieve his stress, coming home with some new treasure to read aloud.

In addition to bookstores, you will need libraries. A full-service public library is one of a community's most precious assets. Get a library card and get to know your children's librarian. If your community does not have a public library, perhaps a community college in your area will have a collection of children's literature that is available for checkout.

More churches are beginning to recognize the importance of a church library. Our church has even developed reading incentive programs for children similar to those of our public library. The range of Christian children's books is growing daily. There are hundreds of well-written, beautifully illustrated books for children that share not only the printed word but the gospel message and Christian ideals. Establishing a library in your church could enable you to build a collection that not only your children but others could use.

Even if you don't have children enrolled in school, the public school library should welcome your interest. In many towns, school and public libraries are a joint venture. They welcome volunteer assistance in many cases, and you will often find them quite willing to purchase your recommendations and requests. The impact of your Christian witness will be more meaningful if it is accompanied by an interest and willingness to roll up your sleeves and work.

WON'T I SPOIL MY CHILD IF I SPEND TOO MUCH TIME READING ALOUD?

This question belongs to the same family of questions as the one often asked by new parents: "Won't I spoil my child if I pick her up every time she cries?" Research at Johns Hopkins University showed that regular, prompt response to an infant's crying resulted in a higher level of attachment between caretaker and baby.[3] The same principle applies to reading aloud. Time spent in reading aloud with your child will result in a higher level of attachment, a sense of security, and the knowledge by your child that you feel she is a worthwhile person with whom to spend time.

The more time you spend reading aloud to your child in

the early years, the less time you will need to spend monitoring and helping your child with homework and school projects once he is of school age. Every hour you spend reading together before the age of five is one hour you won't have to spend working with your teenager over a biology assignment he can't understand. Every hour you spend reading fairy tales together is an hour you won't have to spend helping your daughter decipher Shakespeare for an English class. Children want to be independent and help themselves. Only when we appreciate their dependence and need for constant nurturing and guidance during the early years will they learn the skills and judgment needed to be truly independent.

WHAT IF I HAVE SEVERAL CHILDREN OF DIFFERENT AGES? CAN I READ ALOUD TO ALL OF THEM AT THE SAME TIME?

This depends largely on the ages of the children. If they are close in age, two years or less apart, you can frequently read the same stories to them. However, if you can spend some time alone with each child, especially at bedtime, you will enjoy the unique qualities that each child brings to the read-aloud experience.

An age span of more than two years between children will probably mean two separate sets of read-aloud materials. But you as the parent will be the best judge of what interests your children and holds their attention.

WHEN SHOULD I STOP READING ALOUD?

Continue to read aloud to your children as long as they enjoy listening. Some families continue to read aloud long after their children are independent readers. They may read aloud during illnesses or during long car trips. They read the Bible aloud after the evening meal. One couple I know kept on reading aloud even after their children grew up and moved away. During their vacation trips, they take turns driving and reading aloud to each other. They manage to catch up on recent best sellers in that way.

Your children will let you know when they'd rather read on their own—just as they let you know when they want to walk themselves to school, cut up their own meat, or any of those little milestones that signify a growing independence. Most children reach this stage around third grade, but a year earlier or later would not be unusual. As your child matures, the type of read-aloud selections naturally change. Check chapter five for read-aloud suggestions for older children.

3

The First Three Years

I was a first-time mother. My newborn daughter and I had been home from the hospital only three days. I was more than a little nervous and not quite sure about whether I was doing everything the right way. Far away from family, I was delighted when the PTA president from the school where I had worked called and asked if she could stop by for a visit. I welcomed the opportunity to talk to an experienced "mom." She brought a gift with her as well as some wonderful advice for a new parent.

"I always give books as baby gifts," she said, handing me a colorfully wrapped package. "I hope you'll start reading aloud to Emily right away. I've read aloud to all my children." As a school librarian I was already a believer in reading aloud, but to have a seasoned mother confirm the importance of this practice strengthened my resolve to get started early.

That evening as I rocked my fretful baby asleep, I began reading from the book she had brought. It contained poems and nursery rhymes set off with Tasha Tudor illustrations. That book is still on our shelf while the other baby gifts have been discarded or handed down. Whenever I read the inscription in the flyleaf I think of those early months and the joy that reading aloud brought to me as a new mother. I'm especially grateful to that dedicated mother for her example and the interest she showed in me.

The first three years are special ones for you and your child. They are also among the most important in terms of forming life-long patterns and learning. Your baby can comprehend and learn far beyond what you might imagine. Take advantage of every opportunity to read aloud!

In the first part of this chapter you'll meet four children, ranging in age from six months to two-and-one-half years old. They are composites of many children I've known. Perhaps you'll recognize your own child among them.

There are hundreds of books on the market for these children. To help you choose the best for your child, I'll recommend the best for this age group in the second part of the chapter.

THE CHILDREN

Alex is six months old. His parents have two older children and know that their days of having Alex stay where they put him are nearly over. Only last week, he rolled across the room and pulled over a potted plant.

When he sits in his high chair his favorite game is dropping toys to the floor. His older brothers laugh and clap at his antics, but quickly tire of picking up the rattles. Alex is a very sociable companion and seems to be talking to his brothers as he plays the game. Alex's mother knows that even though he won't begin talking for several months, he is beginning to understand a great deal.

She encourages his older brothers to talk with him—and not with the "baby talk" they seemed to think was appropriate when he was born. Although Alex can't respond in comprehensible words to the conversation around him, his big brown eyes look to each of his brothers as they talk about the snack they are having after school.

Another favorite game of this six month old is hide and seek. His brothers put his blanket in front of their faces and quickly pull it aside, gleefully calling out "peek-a-boo."

The best time for reading stories to Alex is just before naptime or bedtime. He isn't the greatest of cuddlers, but after a bath and bottle, his mother always reads from a favorite rhyme book.

Birth to 3

Karen just celebrated her first birthday. She began walking at nine months, and her insatiable curiosity has already forced her mother to rearrange the house completely.

Only last week she stopped her mother's heart when she climbed from the kitchen chair to the top of the counter. She seemed on her way to the top of the refrigerator when Mom interrupted her.

Although she is an extraordinarily active child, Karen frequently sits motionless while gazing at an object or person. Sometimes she stares out the window, sometimes at her mother, and often at a favorite toy. She seems to be absorbed in learning details about the world around her.

When her father arrives home from work and calls her name from the front door, Karen runs to greet him in response. If she's in a cooperative mood, she will throw him a kiss.

Karen is interested in everything—controls on the stove, water in the toilet bowl, even dust under the bed. She leads her mother on a merry chase from one exciting, exploratory adventure to another. Her mother wisely does not confine her to a playpen, but child-proofs the house wherever possible.

Karen's mother knows how important reading is, and since Karen is fascinated with animals of any kind, they spend time every day reading aloud animal picture books. Mom says the name of the animals and points Karen's finger to the appropriate picture. They make animal sounds and have a good time together. Mom usually can tell when Karen's attention is beginning to wane and puts the books away. They will read again at bedtime, even if only for a short time.

If he weren't packaged in such a small body, the observer would certify that eighteen-month-old **Jason** was a bona fide adolescent. He asserts his own independence and mixes that characteristic with a fair amount of negativism.

He no longer worships his older sister, Sarah, and frequently appears to relish interfering with her model building. At times Jason's only redeeming quality is his ability to engage in delightful conversations. His appealing manner, when he chooses to exhibit it, entrances his grandparents.

Jason loves outdoor activity, and a part of every day is a trip to the local park. He swings, balances on the animal toys, examines the grass, and plays in the sandbox. His mother tries to interest him in watching "Sesame Street," but more that ten minutes of being seated is too much for Jason.

His mother has discovered, however, that reading books with pictures of trucks and fire engines will keep Jason interested for up to twenty minutes. He never tires of looking at the same pictures and naming the machines. Naturally, Jason and Mom have sound effects to accompany the pictures. She continually searches the library and bookstores for different books with trucks, machines, and fire engines. She has found several books with stiff pages that Jason looks at by himself.

Jason loves to hear a story before bedtime. His father is especially good at reading these stories since he fills them with the sound effects that appeal to Jason's exuberant nature. Jason's favorite is the *Ark Full of Animals* where the sound effects are accompanied by animal figure pop-ups on each page. He is already learning about God and hearing simple prayers read aloud.

Maria is a non-stop talker. At two and a half she wants to know *why*. She spends long periods of time building block towers. She enjoys watching "Mister Rogers" while working with her toys. Drawing and pretending to write on paper with crayons are favorite activities also.

Her ability to sit still and concentrate for extended periods makes reading aloud to her a pleasure. She loves all of the books her mother chooses and frequently brings favorites to her mother with a request to "read." Among her most requested titles are *Moses and the Mighty Plague* and *Jonah and the Big Fish.* Maria loves to shop garage sales with her mother and always gets to pick out one or two "bargains" of her own from the book table.

Maria's most oft-requested excursion involves a trip to the animal farm where children can see, talk to, and pet the animals. She would go there every day given the opportunity. Her mom capitalizes on this interest in animals to read every kind of animal story she can find.

Although Maria is intellectually curious, she resists all of her mother's efforts to "teach" her. She is much happier when exploring, questioning, and learning on her own.

She loves routine and becomes very upset if bedtime is not accompanied by at least three stories. She has her own special way of counting the stories and becomes very annoyed if her mother disagrees with her accounting. After a busy day, her mother is grateful that after the three stories Maria will settle down to turn the pages on her own and gradually fall off to sleep surrounded by her books. Her mother always tiptoes in later to remove the books from Maria's bed.

THE CHOICES

As parents we make many choices for our children as they grow. The choices we make for them in their younger years will begin to shape the interests and values that determine the choices they make for themselves as they mature.

You want the books you read to your children to be age-appropriate, well written and illustrated, and an accurate reflection of the Christian beliefs and values that you hold. All of the Christian and secular books included in this chapter and those following meet these criteria. Christian books are indicated by an asterisk. These books will usually be found in your church library or Christian bookstore. Secular books will be found in public libraries and bookstores.

As a parent, I wanted my own children to explore a wide

variety of children's literature, both Christian and secular. However, I knew that I would have to help them select the best of both types. The recommendations that follow will help you do the same.

The read-aloud selections for children from birth to age three will be grouped in nine categories: Bible Story and Prayer Books, Participation Books, Wordless Books, Alphabet Books, Concept Books, Mother Goose and Nursery Rhymes Books, Poetry Books, Picture Books, and Counting Books.

Age categories are often arbitrary. You will find that many of the recommendations in this chapter are also very appropriate for the next age group. For example, *My Book of Bible Rhymes* is first mentioned in this chapter, but I know you will continue reading this charming collection of Biblical stories in verse long after your children have passed their third birthdays. I've chosen to arrange the choices by author since many of our favorite authors have written dozens of excellent read-aloud books. Once you discover an author you like, you can always try different titles.

Bible Story and Prayer Books

This category will be included for each age level, since as children grow their ability to comprehend Bible stories changes. The recommendations here are suitable for that very first Bible story read aloud.

*Colina, Tessa   Illustrated by Vera Gohman
ARK FULL OF ANIMALS
Standard, 1955

This ark-shaped, spiral-bound cardboard book will delight every child. The familiar Noah's Ark story is illustrated with surprise pictures children will find under the lift-up tabs. Although the text is too lengthy for the child under three, a simple retelling of the story while you lift up the tabs will make this a favorite.

*Hague, Michael
A CHILD'S BOOK OF PRAYERS
Holt, Rinehart and Winston, 1985

The traditional childhood prayers are reverently illustrated with five colors, gold borders, and easy-to-read type.

Birth to 3

*Knapp, John II   Illustrated by Dianne Turner Deckert
MY BOOK OF BIBLE RHYMES
David C. Cook, 1987

This unique collection of Bible stories in verse is arranged chronologically from Genesis to Revelation. Knapp is a master poet and his verses will become classics in Christian families. The illustrations are joyful and make the Biblical characters seem real to children. Give this one as a gift to any new parents.

*Lindvall, Ella K.   Illustrated by H. Kent Puckett (Volume 1) and Ken Renczenski (Volume 2)
READ ALOUD BIBLE STORIES   **Volumes 1 and 2**
Moody Press, 1982 and 1985

The stories have been written with the interests and attention span of the two and three year old in mind. The illustrations do an excellent job of telling the stories graphically. Lindvall has resisted the temptation that many Bible story authors fall prey to—that of placing too many words and pictures on each page. These volumes will be favorites of both children and adults.

*Walton, John and Kim   Illustrated by Alice Craig
JONAH AND THE BIG FISH
David C. Cook, 1986

These little Bible story books are gems. (Others in the Early Foundations in the Bible series are *Abraham and His Family, Moses and the Mighty Plague, God and the World He Made, Elijah and the Contest, Daniel and the Lions, Adam and Eve in the Garden,* and *Samuel and the Voice in the Night.*) Colorful illustrations, simple but well-written text, and easy to hold size make these paperbacks a must for every child. If you have occasion to teach a Sunday school lesson on one of these Bible stories, you'll especially appreciate the excellent background notes that help you answer questions children often ask.

Participation Books

These books are appropriate for your very first read-aloud experience. The books are often made of cloth or heavy cardboard so that little fingers cannot damage the pages. The illustrations and text are simple. The books are usually small.

*Bennett, Marian   Illustrated by Mary Ann Dorr
I GO TO CHURCH
Standard, 1985

One of the "My Shape Book" series, this board book is shaped like a church steeple. The text and illustrations are appropriate for the very young child. Other titles in the series include *Shapes and Things, My Family and Friends, Animals in the Ark, Bible Story Favorites,* and *God's Rainbow of Colors.*

*Bracken, Carolyn
THE BABY JESUS
Thomas Nelson, 1985

Part of the Tuck-a-Toy series, this cloth book has been designed to develop manual dexterity as your baby learns about some "special babies." Others in the series are *The Baby Moses, The Baby Bear,* and *The Special Baby.* In each book, the featured baby is attached with a colorful ribbon and can be tucked into a special place provided on the front cover. Young ones delight in putting Baby Jesus or Baby Moses in and out of their special beds.

Bruna, Dick
I CAN READ
Price/Stern/Sloan, 1984

If your toddler is eager to associate words and pictures, this little book is perfect. Black and white line drawings are highlighted with primary colors to illustrate simple words. Bruna has written many of these little books (*I Can Read More, The Apple, I Know About Shapes*). If you like his style, you'll have many titles to choose from.

Burningham, John
THE RABBIT
Thomas Y. Crowell, 1975

You'll want to read every one of John Burningham's books to your child during the first three years. Each one has soft drawings, simple but beautifully written text, and best of all—an undeniable appeal to the younger child. *The Baby, The Friend, The Blanket,* and *The Snow* all contain the same little boy and show him solving the problems common to young children.

*Evans, Linden
GOD MADE ALL THE COLORS
Lion, 1979

Buy this series as part of your baby's first exposure to books. *(God Made Them All, Who Made Friends? Who Made Mothers and Fathers? Great and Small,* and *Bright and Beautiful.)* The illustrations are whimsical, the colors are brilliant, and the text is simple, but meaningful.

Kunhardt, Dorothy
PAT THE BUNNY
Golden, 1962

No list of participation books would be complete without this classic. A popular gift, it appeals to the child's senses. Patting the furry bunny, smelling the scented flower, and playing peek-a-boo with the child in the book involve your child in many ways.

Lionni, Leo
WHO
Pantheon, 1983

This wordless board book is part of a series. Other titles are, of course, *What, Where,* and *When.* The characteristic Lionni mice drawings are found on each page with a person, object, location, or event. The child and parent can together discover who, what, where, or when.

*Tangvald, Christine Harder   Illustrated by June Goldsborough
MY OWN SPECIAL BODY
David C. Cook, 1985

Part of the I Am Special Series *(I Can Talk to God, When I Am Sick, Me Myself, and I, My Family Is Special, My Friends Are Special, Oh, Yes! Oh, No!,* and *Good For Me),* these lightweight board books are designed to develop your child's awareness that he is a unique creation of God. Each book is written about a different child and the illustrations are charming.

*Wells, Mick, Illustrator
GOD LOVES ME
Lion Publishing, 1981

Another excellent board book series comes from England. Although some words are distinctively British (Mum and Gran), the concepts, illustrations, and text are perfect for that first read-aloud experience. The message in *God Loves Me* is elegantly expressed in both pictures and words.

Wordless Books

Wordless books allow the child's imagination to create a story of her own. The illustrations become the focal point and the story can have a variety of interpretations depending on your mood.

Hutchins, Pat
CHANGES, CHANGES
Macmillan, 1971

Does your child enjoy playing with colorful wooden blocks? If so, he'll enjoy this clever wordless book. A pair of wooden dolls rearrange blocks on each page as they build their home, put out a fire with their block fire engine, and eventually sail away in their block boat.

*Spier, Peter
NOAH'S ARK
Doubleday, 1977

The Biblical story of Noah and the Ark is meticulously illustrated by Peter Spier. Examine the drawings carefully to see Noah cope with a hive of bees and a recalcitrant donkey. My favorite illustration shows the inside of the ark after Noah and his menagerie have exited. Quite a mess! A more recent title is *Book of Jonah*.

Alphabet Books

Alphabet books are designed to teach the alphabet. But they have other purposes as well. You and your child can learn to appreciate a variety of different artists as you compare the different ways they have presented the alphabet. While learning the alphabet you'll increase vocabulary and enhance language development. Alphabet books comprise a fascinating part of children's literature.

Chess, Victoria
ALFRED'S ALPHABET WALK
Greenwillow, 1979

Young Alfred is charged with learning his alphabet and decides to take a walk to help him learn. Along the way he encounters a "group of gray gorillas that were all grinning," and "a tortoise and a toad who were trying to toss tiddleywinks into a top hat." If your child loves tongue twisters and word play, this alphabet book will delight him. The illustrations are charming. Alfred the oppossum will become an immediate favorite.

Fujikawa, Gyo
A TO Z PICTURE BOOK
Grosset & Dunlap, 1974

Fujikawa is a magnificent artist. You could spend hours with this book and never see all he has created. Some letters of the alphabet are illustrated with a double-page spread in full color. Other letters are shown with black and white line drawings of many different objects. Favorites at our house were "B is for busy babies!" and "D is for dreams, all kinds of dreams, dangerous and delicious ones . . . dreadful . . . delightful . . . and disgusting ones!"

Hague, Kathleen   Illustrated by Michael Hague
ALPHABEARS
Holt, Rinehart & Winston, 1983

Imagine twenty-six different teddy bears, each with a unique personality. There are male and female bears and each one is shown with a full page painting and a charming rhyme. These bears are the most lovable I've ever seen!

Wildsmith, Brian
BRIAN WILDSMITH'S ABC
Franklin Watts, 1962

Any of Wildsmith's books are works of art. His drawings are complex with unusual colors, but every child should be exposed to his style and encouraged to compare and contrast his work with other ABC books.

Concept Books

Reading aloud from this category of books will give you countless opportunities to teach your child while having fun.

A concept is defined as an "abstract notion." Through these entertaining read-alouds your child will begin to understand the concepts of love, God, sharing, family, prayer, shapes, colors, and ideas such as over, under, through, and around.

Birth to 3

*Anderson, Debby
GOD IS WITH ME
Standard, A Happy Day Book, 1984

Happy Day Books are the Christian counterpart to the Golden Book. Their distinctive shapes and board covers make them easy to read aloud. Other titles include *Sharing Makes Me Happy, My ABC Zoo Book,* and *Saying Thank You Makes Me Happy.* Although inexpensive, they are colorful and sturdy. When your child begins choosing his own books to buy, you will have over sixty titles to choose from.

*Blanton, Mary Thornton   Illustrated by Helen Endres
GOD MADE IT ALL
Scripture Press, SonFlower Books, 1983

This hardcover book is particularly well written. In easy-to-read rhyme, the author is able to convey the concept that God has made all things. Your child will want to hear this one read aloud many times and you will have a good time together naming the colorfully illustrated creations of God.

Carle, Eric
MY VERY FIRST BOOK OF WORDS
Thomas Y. Crowell, 1974

You can have fun learning ten new words as you match the word on the top of the page with pictures on the bottom. Illustrations are simple and colorful Carle classics. There are several others in the series including *My Very First Book of Shapes.*

Crews, Donald
FREIGHT TRAIN
Greenwillow, 1978

Is your child fascinated by a passing train? If so he'll love to turn the pages in *Freight Train*. The pictures and print are clean and sized for the pre-schooler. He'll learn about colors, varieties of train cars, and the concepts by, through, and over. The train seems to be moving as you read the book. Other Crews books for the child fascinated by vehicles are *School Bus* and *Truck*.

*Gunn, Robin Jones   Illustrated by Kathy Mitter
BILLY 'N' BEAR VISIT GRANDPA AND GRANDMA
Concordia, 1985

The simple text and soft illustrations relate an every day experience in the life of Billy. The best part of this series (*Billy 'n' Bear Go to the Doctor, Billy 'n' Bear Go to a Birthday Party, Billy 'n' Bear Go to the Grocery Store, Billy 'n' Bear Go to Church,* and *Billy 'n' Bear Go to Sunday School*) is the simple prayer contained in each story. Billy is shown with his Grandpa and Grandma while the text simply states: "God, thank You for my Grandpa and Grandma. I love them very much. Amen." These books introduce prayer in the most natural of ways.

Hoban, Tana
DIG, DRILL, DUMP, FILL
Greenwillow, 1975

Full page black and white photographs of machines of many kinds will fascinate your inquisitive toddler. Hoban's other books—*Shapes and Things; Circles, Triangles, and Squares; Over, Under, and Through; Round and Round and Round;* and *Push-Pull, Empty-Full* are also ideal for teaching concepts. If you enjoy photography yourself, you will appreciate Hoban's work.

Kalan, Robert Illustrated by Donald Crews
BLUE SEA
Greenwillow, 1979

The concepts of big and little are delightfully presented, and before long you'll find your toddler "reading" along with you. The repetition of phrases gives a poetic feel to the text, and the deep blue pages with brightly colored letters and fish put the reader right into the ocean.

Pienkowski, Jan
TIME
Julian Messner, 1980

If your toddler is fascinated with clocks, pick up this small book that contains clocks showing different times and events throughout the day and night.

Reiss, John J.
COLORS
Bradbury Press, 1971

This is the best of the color books. You'll have a wonderful time looking at all of the "things to eat, things to wear, and things to pat" in vivid colors.

Rockwell, Anne
PLANES
E.P. Dutton, 1985

Is your child interested in all kinds of planes, trucks, boats, or cars? Anne Rockwell has written the perfect books to satisfy even the most curious. Bright watercolors and large type will make these favorites of all children. Other titles in the series include *Trucks, Boats,* and *Cars.*

Scarry, Richard
BEST WORD BOOK EVER
Western, 1963

Tiny drawings and busy pages are Richard Scarry's trademark. But children of all ages never seem to tire of asking, "What's this?" With this book your child can learn dozens of new words and little fingers can point to more than 1400 different objects illustrated in full color. Other titles are: *What Do People Do All Day?*, *Richard Scarry's ABC Word Book*, and *Richard Scarry's Great Big Air Book*.

Rojankovsky, Feodor
ANIMALS ON THE FARM
Alfred A. Knopf, 1967

The drawings done in soft greens and browns cover every farm animal you're likely to encounter, plus several not so likely ones— storks, peacocks, and swans. Each full page drawing is accompanied by the animal name in large print. This book is perfect for the child who never tires of looking at animal pictures.

Mother Goose and Nursery Rhymes
You probably won't need more than one Mother Goose treasury unless you're a serious collector. So take your time and browse through several before you make a selection.

deAngeli, Marguerite
MARGUERITE DE ANGELI'S BOOK OF NURSERY AND MOTHER GOOSE RHYMES
Doubleday, 1954

With 376 rhymes included, this anthology is one of the largest. A Caldecott Honor Book, the soft, delicate illustrations in pastels never overpower the rhymes.

Hague, Michael
MOTHER GOOSE
Holt, Rinehart and Winston, 1984

This collection of classic nursery rhymes is beautifully illustrated in a soft, old-fashioned style. Since there is only one rhyme and illustration per page, the volume is especially appropriate for the younger child. An index of first lines is very helpful.

Greenaway, Kate
A MOTHER GOOSE TREASURY
Avenel Books, 1966

This small volume of selected Mother Goose rhymes is magically illustrated in the Greenaway fashion. If you have fond memories of Mother Goose, you'll want this one to share with your child.

Potter, Beatrix
BEATRIX POTTER'S NURSERY RHYME BOOK
Frederick Warne, 1984

The type and the illustrations preserve the flavor of the original Potter work. If you like your Mother Goose with a traditional flavor, then add this one to your collection.

Wildsmith, Brian
BRIAN WILDSMITH'S MOTHER GOOSE
Franklin Watts, 1964

The expressions on the faces of your favorite Mother Goose characters are the best part of Brian Wildsmith's rendition of Mother Goose. Add to that his irrepressible colors and wonderful, watercolor wash backgrounds and you have a collector's item.

Poetry

Poems are word pictures, written to capture the feeling or mood of a certain time or place. When a new snow has just fallen, take the poetry book from the shelf and read A.A. Milne's "The More It Snows." As you drive over the highway to Grandmother's house for Thanksgiving day, the lines "Over the river and through the wood, to grandmother's house we go," just beg to be recited. One or two poetry collections belong in every family's library.

Frank, Josette   Illustrated by Eloise Wilkins
POEMS TO READ TO THE VERY YOUNG
Random House, 1982

This should be the first poetry collection you buy. Expressive illustrations by Eloise Wilkins bring to life the poetry of such favorites as A.A. Milne, Christina Rosetti, and Robert Louis Stevenson. However, there are many poems included by more contemporary poets like Jack Prelutsky as well.

Prelutsky, Jack   Illustrated by Arnold Lobel
THE RANDOM HOUSE BOOK OF POETRY FOR CHILDREN
Random House, 1983

This anthology creatively groups poetry into sections. Titles such as "Nature Is . . . " and "Alphabet Stew" let the reader know what kinds of poems are found in each section. The editor, Jack Prelutsky, an outstanding poet in his own right, has written a special poem for each section. Arnold Lobel, well know for his *Frog and Toad* series, has contributed hundreds of drawings, sketches, and paintings.

Picture Books

The simple stories contained in this list can be read over and over. They will be enjoyed as much on their tenth or twentieth reading as on the first. That is the true test of a read-aloud picture book. If your child of two or three enjoys longer and more complex stories, look ahead to Chapter Four where dozens of picture books are listed.

Brown, Margaret Wise   Illustrated by Clement Hurd
GOOD NIGHT MOON
Harper & Row, 1947

A perfect story for bedtime read-aloud. The rhyming words and delightful illustrations will help you transition your child from busy activities to a quiet and restful bedtime. Other favorites by Brown include *The Little Fireman, Little Fur Family,* and *The Runaway Bunny.*

Domanska, Janina
I SAW A SHIP A-SAILING
Macmillan, 1972

Wonderful illustrations bring this nursery rhyme to life.

Eastman, P.D.
ARE YOU MY MOTHER?
Random House, Beginner Book, 1960

Although this title is part of the "I Can Read It All By Myself" series of "Beginner Books," the storyline is one that will delight your two or three year old. A baby bird falls out of the nest and tries to find his mother. Before he finds his way back to the nest he asks the question "Are you my mother?" of a kitten, hen, cow, and even a steam shovel. Your young one will delight in knowing who the bird's real mother is before the bird finds out on his own.

Flack, Marjorie
ASK MR. BEAR
Macmillan, 1932

Danny needs a birthday present for his mother. After consulting Mrs. Hen, Mrs. Goose, and numerous other barnyard animals, Danny finally goes to Mr. Bear who comes up with a surprising idea. You'll have plenty of opportunity to do your "animal impressions" with this old favorite.

Ginsburg, Mirra   Illustrated by Jose & Ariane Aruego
THE CHICK AND THE DUCKLING
Macmillan, 1972

Bold, colorful drawings illustrate the simple text of this Russian tale. Chick and Duckling hatch into the world at the same time. They play "anything you can do, I can do also," until Chick discovers that Duckling can swim. The predictable results will delight your toddler. Another excellent folktale is *The Strongest One of All.*

Hale, Sarah Josepha   Illustrated by Tomie dePaola
MARY HAD A LITTLE LAMB
Holiday House, 1984

Mary's little lamb comes to life under the brush of the multi-talented Tomie dePaola. Each illustration is a masterpiece of delightful, historically accurate detail. The small child who has heard this rhyme many times will love hearing you read this book aloud.

Hutchins, Patricia
ROSIE'S WALK
Macmillan, 1968

Your child will never tire of hearing *Rosie's Walk.* Rosie the hen goes for a walk never realizing that a fox is close behind her. Your pre-schooler will howl with glee as the fox runs into several misadventures while Rosie gets back home in time for dinner unharmed. Hutchins has a knack for writing and illustrations that entrance the preschooler. Other favorites are *Happy Birthday, Sam* and *Goodnight Owl.*

Johnson, Crockett
HAROLD AND THE PURPLE CRAYON
Harper & Row, 1955

Toddlers will be mesmerized as Harold creates pictures with his purple crayon. They will want to read this one over and over as they try to figure out just how Harold is able to do whatever he wants with only his imagination and a purple crayon. Just make sure you keep those crayons under lock and key after you've read this one. Other titles in the series are *Harold's Trip to the Sky, Harold's ABC,* and *Harold's Circus.*

Krauss, Ruth   Illustrated by Crockett Johnson
THE CARROT SEED
Harper & Row, 1945

This is the perfect story to read aloud when you and your child plant that first seed together. The little boy in this simple story has faith that his seed will come up even though his family is certain it won't.

Lenski, Lois
DAVY GOES PLACES
Henry Z. Walck, Inc., 1961

The Davy books are small enough for the toddler to hold and look at on his own. Simple illustrations and text tell of every day happenings in a little boy's life. They were favorites of my children. Other titles are: *Davy Goes Places, Davy and His Dog, Big Little Davy, A Dog Came to School, Surprise for Davy,* and *Davy's Day.*

Martin, Bill, Jr.   Illustrated by Eric Carle
BROWN BEAR, BROWN BEAR, WHAT DO YOU SEE?
Holt, Rinehart and Winston, 1983

This title combines all of the elements a successful book for the toddler needs—bright illustrations, simple text, and an elegant concept. You will find before long that your toddler has memorized the words and is "reading" with you. Brown Bear, redbird, yellow duck, and blue horse will soon become bedtime favorites at your house.

Misha
THE THREE LITTLE KITTENS
Golden Press, 1942

Little Golden Books have delighted several generations of children. They must be purchased selectively, but they offer an inexpensive read-aloud that children can handle and enjoy for years. The illustrations that accompany this version of the favorite nursery rhyme are charming. Other Golden Book favorites at our house were: *We Help Daddy, The Little Red Hen, Animal Counting Book,* and *Baby Animals.*

*Ward, Alton
10 PENNIES FOR JESUS
Concordia, 1986

What can the pennies your child places in the offering basket do for Jesus? This charming story will tell him. I especially liked the realistic illustrations of pennies in the basket. They brought back wonderful memories of Sunday school offerings.

Zolotow, Charlotte
WAKE UP AND GOOD NIGHT
Harper & Row, 1971

There's no better way to say "good morning" or "good night" than reading this poem to morning and evening. The morning illustrations are bright and cheery. The evening illustrations are wonderfully dark and shadowy. Another excellent Zolotow book for the infant-toddler is *But Not Billy,* the story of a little boy saying his first word.

Counting Books

Children are captivated by numbers. They love to count. This selection of counting books will give you all kinds of things to count—animals, lollipops, birthday candles, and even radishes. An early introduction to numbers will make math seem fun when school begins.

Brown, Marc
AN ANIMAL COUNTING BOOK
Little, Brown and Company, 1976

If your child is held spellbound by animals of any kind, this counting book with brown-tone illustrations will surely delight her. Each animal in the number sets to twenty has a slightly different personality. You will have fun discovering just how each animal differs from the others.

Carle, Eric
1, 2, 3 TO THE ZOO
Collins World, 1968

Animals are a sure-fire subject for a counting book, and in Eric Carle's version they are part of a train going to the zoo. If your toddler is going to the zoo, be sure to read this counting book both before and after your trip.

Crews, Donald
TEN BLACK DOTS
Greenwillow, 1986

"What can you do with ten black dots?" Donald Crews, in his inimitable graphic style, shows you. One dot can make a sun, three dots a snowman's face, and eight dots the wheels on a train.

Hoban, Tana
COUNT AND SEE
Macmillan, 1972

This prize-winning photographer has put together a counting book that emphasizes real objects with which children can identify. The photos are black and white and accompanied by white dots on black pages so that children can practice their counting in several ways.

Hutchins, Pat
1 HUNTER
Greenwillow, 1982

A lone hunter sets out for the jungle, and along the way he encounters 2 elephants, 3 giraffes, 7 crocodiles, and a variety of other jungle creatures. A creative contribution to your counting book collection.

Oxenbury, Helen
HELEN OXENBURY'S NUMBERS OF THINGS
Delacorte Press, 1967

You'll never outgrow your need for counting books. This one has pictures illustrating the numbers 20, 30, 40, and 50 for those children who are interested in counting farther than ten. Oxenbury's illustrations are marvelous, and her choice of subjects ranges from acrobats to ladybugs.

4

Off
To
School

Sending your children off to school is a scary experience. I remember when mine started preschool and kindergarten. Suddenly they weren't all mine anymore. I wasn't part of their experiences during every waking minute. I no longer controlled how they spent their time or what they learned. Suddenly the time we'd spent together in those first three years seemed overwhelmingly important. But it was over! Now I just had to trust and pray that when away from home, they would value and remember the lessons we'd learned together.

I spent two or three days contemplating this dreadful separation. Then I went out for breakfast and prepared to enjoy the flip side of the coin that their attending school brought to our lives. My children made new friends, they were able to listen to others read stories aloud, and they learned all kinds of new skills and ideas. Books were a wonderful resource to our family in these beginning-school years. Reading aloud together gave us reason to sit down and talk about school, friends, problems, and the meaning of life. They gave us a way to spend time together and keep in touch.

In this chapter you will meet several children between ages four and seven who are in these beginning-school years. Their attitudes about formal reading instruction are beginning to be formed and they are learning new skills every day. 65

Perhaps you'll recognize your own child among the group.

In the second part of the chapter you will find books which are recommended for reading aloud to children in this crucial age span of four through seven years of age.

THE CHILDREN

Jeremy is four years old. His father appreciates his exuberant and bold nature, but his mom is constantly setting limits and reminding Jeremy that he's only four years old and can't ride his bicycle down the front steps. Jeremy is a study in contrasts. He often walks down the street to play with a close friend, carefully remaining on the sidewalk as per his mother's instructions. However, in an instant he can turn into a verbal whirlwind and tell his mother he hates her.

Jeremy attends church preschool and loves the vigorous physical activity that is part of the program. He builds enthusiastically with big blocks and plays vivid imaginary games with his closest friend, John. He loves the Bible stories the teacher reads each day, especially the ones that involve action and adventure.

Jeremy's favorite outdoor activity involves water. He loves to "paint" the driveway and sidewalk with an old brush and bucket. He will often paint elaborate designs and letters on the concrete.

Jeremy has a wonderful sense of humor and particularly enjoys the books his parents read that have ridiculous plots. He loves detailed drawings and is able to name all of the pictures in his alphabet and word books. Jeremy's favorite author is Dr. Seuss.

Jeremy is beginning to have a strong sense of the difference between good and bad. He knows that God wants him to be good and prays with his mom or dad each night. His prayers are expansive, asking God to bless each of his friends, his grandparents, and even his pet frog.

Adam has just begun kindergarten. At five years old, he

loves everyone, especially his mother and his kindergarten teacher. He spends a great deal of time talking and tells his mother all about what goes on each morning at school. They are cutting, pasting, playing, singing, stringing, dancing, running, and jumping. He wants to duplicate all of his school activities at home.

Ages 4-7

Although he has always loved stories being read aloud to him, now that he's five he can't get enough reading aloud. Adam's mom shares this happy task with her older children. Adam has many close friends, but Mom wisely invites only one at a time to play. Sharing friends is still a difficult assignment for this five year old.

When he misbehaves, Adam responds well to time-out in his bedroom. Five or ten minutes away from the family usually results in a contrite, cooperative child.

Although Adam falls asleep quickly after bedtime stories, he frequently wakes up with nightmares. His parents are careful to read quiet, friendly stories before bedtime. They always end their nighttime story hour with a prayer from Adam's favorite book of prayers and ask God to watch over Adam while he is sleeping. Adam asks many questions about God and believes that He is responsible for everything. The death of Adam's grandfather generated many questions, and his parents were grateful to have a book like *What Happens When We Die?* to read aloud to him.

When she was five years of age **Elizabeth** was a delight. Now that she has turned six, she has changed into a real crybaby. School is too hard; her friends don't like her; she doesn't like any of the food served at meals; her feelings are always bruised. Loving Elizabeth takes lots of patience and sensitivity. Surprisingly, her teacher at school sees none of this negative behavior, although Elizabeth does have a difficult time sitting still and remaining quiet for an entire morning at school.

But Elizabeth's mood can change quickly. When she can forget about the emotional ups and downs of being six, her relationship with the world and life is enthusiastic. She loves to read, write, and draw. She talks non-stop and has strong opinions about her likes and dislikes. She is very curious about babies and how they've come to be. She wants to know about death and where people go after they die.

She is an enthusiastic participant in church and Sunday school. She loves to sing and has memorized many hymns and choruses. She enjoys looking over her Sunday school papers and asks to have the stories read aloud to her.

Elizabeth is learning to read in school. She brings mountains of papers home each week and carefully explains her handiwork to her younger brother. She would like him to play school, but at three his attention span doesn't satisfy the teacher in Elizabeth.

Her mother sometimes feels that a small tornado has passed through the kitchen when Elizabeth comes home from school. Once she has had a snack and shared the woes of her day, Elizabeth's bright and sunny nature returns. Going to school all day is definitely hard work.

Seth is seven years old. A new baby has just arrived in his family, and Seth is a big help to his mother. He empties the garbage, makes his own bed, and picks up his room. His mother was concerned about how Seth would respond to a new family member, but he has assumed the big brother role with ease.

Seth is an excellent reader and enjoys books about real boys his own age who do exciting things. Animals, space travel, and strange bugs also intrigue him. During weekly trips to the library, he checks out several books he can read by himself. He also has several magazine subscriptions that his grandparents gave him—*Ranger Rick, National Geographic World,* and *Electric Company.* He has carefully organized them in his bedroom and regularly rearranges and looks at them.

Seth is preoccupied with the idea of heaven, probably because of his interest in space. He wants to know where it is, how God gets there, and how is it possible that God can see everything and be everywhere while remaining in heaven.

Perhaps Seth's most disagreeable trait at age seven is his need for perfection. He dislikes mistakes in himself and in his family and friends. He doesn't take correction well and often tries to cover up his errors. He frequently dawdles while dressing himself in the morning, and his mother has come up with a timer system that seems to keep him engaged in the task of getting dressed.

Ages 4-7

With the arrival of a new baby, there has been less time for reading aloud, but Seth's teacher has a contest going at school, so Seth is very motivated and reminds his mom or dad daily that he needs to read with them.

THE CHOICES

The choices from which to make your read-aloud selections for children between the ages of four and seven will be grouped into the following categories: Bible Story and Scriptural Application Books; Picture Books; Books for the Independent Reader; Concept, Counting, and Alphabet Books for the Older Child; Folk and Fairy Tales; and Poetry. Christian books in each category are indicated with an asterisk.

Bible Story And Scriptural Application Books

These books will be especially helpful as you guide your children spiritually and attempt to answer the many questions and concerns they have about God and living the Christian life.

*Batchelor, Mary   Editor
THE LION BOOK OF CHILDREN'S PRAYERS
Lion, 1977

A comprehensive collection of over 200 children's prayers. This volume could be used as a book of poetry, as a family devotional, or simply as a read aloud at special times. The illustrations and photos are outstanding.

---

*Beers, V. Gilbert and Ronald A.   Illustrated by Reint DeJong
WALKING WITH JESUS
Here's Life Publishers, 1984
An exceptionally well-illustrated book that details the life of Jesus in one-page stories.

---

*Cioni, Ray & Sally
THE DROODLES TEN COMMANDMENTS STORYBOOK
David C. Cook, 1983

The "far-out" creatures with weird names, strange shapes, and vivid colors created by Ray and Sally Cioni will definitely attract the attention of your children. And while you have their attention, the Droodles will illustrate how Biblical truths apply to every day life. This series is most unusual, but very appealing to today's child. Another title in the series is *The Droodles Storybook of Proverbs.*

---

*Colson, Charles with William Coleman
Illustrated by Gwen Connelly
GUESS WHO'S AT MY PARTY
David C. Cook, 1986

Although your child won't realize who Charles Colson is, the series he has co-authored will impress you with its straightforward presentation of Biblical truth through stories about real kids. Other titles in the series are: *Being Good Isn't Easy, Trouble in the School Yard,* and *Watch Out for Becky.*

---

*Egermeier, Elsie   Revised by Arlene S. Hall
EGERMEIER'S BIBLE STORY BOOK
Warner Press, 1969

When choosing a Bible storybook, an important consideration is both the quality of the writing and the adherence to Biblical truth. The paperback version of this classic (first printed in 1922) has both. Excellent illustrations and brief, but well-written, stories that children will enjoy make this a must for your family bookshelf. The index of stories is especially helpful. Other titles by Egermeier include *Egermeier's Favorite Bible Stories* (thirty stories adapted for younger readers), *Egermeier's Picture-Story Life of Jesus* (stories of the life of Christ adapted from the big story book), and *Picture Story Bible ABC Book*.

Ages 4-7

*Hill, Dave   Illustrated by Betty Wind
THE BOY WHO GAVE HIS LUNCH AWAY
Concordia, Arch Books 1967

The Arch paperback Bible stories in rhyme have withstood the test of time. Children adore them! There are now over 100 in the series by different authors and illustrators. Read through the ones you plan to purchase for quality of writing and illustration. Other favorites in our family included *The Boy with a Sling, The Braggy King of Babylon,* and *The Lame Man Who Walked Again.* Some of the individual stories have been collected in two hardcover collections: *Children of the Old Testament* and *Children of the New Testament.*

*Jackson, Dave   Illustrated by Susan Lexa
SHY BUT NOT TOO SHY
David C. Cook, 1986

If your child is experiencing a difficult situation, the Storybook for Caring Parents series may provide an opportunity for you to help her using a read-aloud experience. In addition to three different stories that illustrate aspects of a problem, a section for parents is included. Other titles in the series include *Unfair but Not Too Unfair, Scared but Not Too Scared, Tired but Not Too Tired, Bored but Not Too Bored, Angry but Not Too Angry, Stubborn but Not Too Stubborn,* and *Disappointed but Not Too Disappointed.*

*Lindvall, Ella K.   Illustrated by Paul Turnbaugh
THE BIBLE ILLUSTRATED FOR LITTLE CHILDREN
Moody Press, 1985

One page stories with soft and lovely illustrations.

*Marxhausen, Joanne   Illustrated by Benjamin Marxhausen
3 IN 1 (A PICTURE OF GOD)
Concordia, 1973

The Biblical truth of the Trinity is eloquently presented in picture form with simple text.

*Murphy, Elspeth Campbell   Illustrated by Jane E. Nelson
SOMETIMES I GET LONELY: PSALM 42 FOR CHILDREN
David C. Cook, 1981

In the David and I series (there are fifteen titles altogether), the psalmist David and the child talk to God about their problems. And God answers—through the inspiration of the Psalms. The illustrations are particularly well done, the writing natural and unpretentious. Titles include: *Sometimes I Get Scared; Where Are You, God?; What Can I Say to You God?; Sometimes I'm Good, Sometimes I'm Bad; Everybody, Shout Hallelujah!; Sometimes I Get Mad; Sometimes I Have to Cry; Sometimes I Need to Be Hugged; It's My Birthday, God; Make Way for the King; I'm Listening, God; Sometimes I Think "What If?"; Sometimes Everything Feels Just Right;* and *God, You Fill Us Up With Joy.*

*Murphy, Elspeth Campbell   Illustrated by Jane E. Nelson
GOD CARES WHEN I'M SORRY
David C. Cook, 1983

The God's Word in My Heart Series is designed to help your child memorize Scripture and understand it in a meaningful way. The fifteen stories about "real" children are well written, and the notes to parents and teachers are especially helpful. Other titles in the series include *God Cares When I'm Worried, God Cares When I'm Disappointed, God Cares When I Wish I Weren't Me, God Cares When I'm Thankful, God Cares When I'm Punished, God Cares When Someone Else Has More,* and *God Cares When I Don't Feel Good.*

*NOW YOU CAN READ STORIES FROM THE BIBLE
Nelson, 1983

Stories in large print that the advanced beginning reader can handle on his own.

---

*Nystrom, Carolyn   Illustrated by Wayne A. Hanna
WHO IS JESUS?
Moody Press, 1980

Ages
4-7

The Children's Bible Basics series explains Christian concepts and principles in a way that children can understand. The text is based on scriptural references and the colorful illustrations and meaningful applications to the child's own life are outstanding. Other titles in the series include *What Is Prayer?*, *Why Do I Do Things Wrong?*, *What Is a Christian?*, *The Holy Spirit in Me*, *What Is the Bible?*, *What Is the Church?*, *Growing Jesus' Way*, *What Happens When We Die?*, and *Jesus Is No Secret.*

---

*READ 'N GROW PICTURE BIBLE
Sweet Publishing Co., 1984

Each page contains six excellent illustrations captioned with one or two simple sentences that tell the story. For children who enjoy many illustrations with their Bible stories, this volume is perfect.

---

*Tangvald, Christine Harder
Illustrated by Frances and Richard Hook
A CHILD'S BOOK OF PRAYERS
David C. Cook, 1987

This collection of simple children's prayers is beautifully illustrated. The prayers are well written and the illustrations are warm and reverent. A book you will want to have in your permanent collection.

Picture Books

Picture books tell a simple story and are accompanied by colorful illustrations. The true test of a good picture book is its enduring readability. You'll soon learn which authors in this category have a knack for catching the interest and attention of both you and your children. Then you can find other titles by that same author. That's why the books are arranged alphabetically by author. I've selected those authors and titles that have survived the read-aloud test either in our home or in the various classrooms and libraries in which I've worked. However, there are hundreds of others from which to choose. My list is in no way meant to be inclusive.

*Baker, Sanna Anderson   Illustrated by Tomie dePaola
WHO'S A FRIEND OF THE WATER-SPURTING WHALE?
David C. Cook, 1987

The sea, the sky, the land, and the creatures point Old Testament character Job to the all-powered and all-knowing God when Job struggles to understand the meaning of life. God reminds him who is in control through a series of revealing questions. The magnificent, full-color illustrations and hand lettering can be appreciated for their beauty alone. But the book is more than a work of art. The poetry and art celebrate the Biblical concept of God's care for his creatures. A must for you and your child to read-aloud over and over.

Bemelmans, Ludwig
MADELINE'S RESCUE
Viking Press, 1951

Madeline and her eleven friends attend a boarding school in Paris. Her stories are told in wonderful rhymes that children love and soon can memorize. The continental touch is unmistakable, and you'll enjoy all of Madeline's adventures: *Madeline, Madeline and the Bad Hat, Madeline and the Gypsies,* and *Madeline's Christmas.*

Bishop, Claire and Kurt Wiese
FIVE CHINESE BROTHERS
Coward-McCann, 1938

You probably have this one memorized from your own childhood. The five Chinese brothers have amazing powers and use them to save their first brother's life.

Ages 4-7

Brunhoff, Jean de
THE STORY OF BABAR, THE LITTLE ELEPHANT
Random House, 1961

Babar is a rather sophisticated French elephant. His stories have been translated from the French and the titles number over two dozen. I never particularly enjoyed reading them aloud, but my children loved Babar and always chose them when we visited the library. Try one or two and judge for yourself.

Burton, Virginia Lee
MIKE MULLIGAN AND HIS STEAM SHOVEL
Houghton Mifflin, 1939

Mike Mulligan and his steam shovel Mary Anne should be part of everyone's childhood experience. The author had a superb under-standing of children and many of her stories are well-loved classics: *Katy and the Big Snow* and *The Little House*.

Carle, Eric
THE VERY HUNGRY CATERPILLAR
Puffin, 1984

Even the most reluctant reader will become involved with Eric Carle's books. *The Very Hungry Caterpillar* eats his way through all kinds of fruit, leaving holes in the pages for curious fingers. *The Grouchy Ladybug* makes his way from page to page as both the type and page sizes increase. Other Carle books have different engaging surprises not found in the typical read aloud: *The Mixed-Up Chameleon* and *The Secret Birthday Message*.

Carrick, Carol   Illustrated by Donald Carrick
THE ACCIDENT
Houghton Mifflin, 1976

This series *(The Foundling, Lost in the Storm, Sleep Out,* and *Dark and Full of Secrets)* is for the child who is ready for a longer read-aloud story with a more complex plot. Christopher is a real boy who confronts many of the realities of life in a believable and interesting way.

Cohen, Miriam   Illustrated by Lillian Hoban
WHEN WILL I READ?
Greenwillow, 1977

The author has a knack for describing the anxieties that beset the average first grader. She reassures children that they are special and that they "can" do it. Other stories in the same vein are: *First Grade Takes a Test, Lost in the Museum,* and *No Good in Art.*

*DePaola, Tomie
THE CHRISTMAS PAGEANT
Winston Press, 1981

This charming paperback retelling of the Christmas story contains all the ingredients for putting on your own Christmas pageant— puppets to color and mount with sticks or flannel. This story could become a holiday read-aloud tradition at your house with very little effort. DePaola's re-telling of *The Story of the Three Wise Kings* is beautifully done, also. He has chosen to paint the mother and child in a style reminiscent of Romanesque painting, a much different interpretation than is usually found. *The Friendly Beasts* completes the trilogy of outstanding Christmas books that DePaola has contributed to our enjoyment of the Christmas season.

*Dotts, Mary Ann   Illustrated by Paul Zepelinsky
WHEN JESUS WAS BORN
Abingdon, 1979

A beautiful rendering of the Christmas story. The line drawings are attractive and the repetition of key words on each page makes this a wonderful read aloud.

Delton, Judy Illustrated by Lillian Hoban
I'M TELLING YOU NOW
E.P. Dutton, 1983

Although Artie's mother told him never to cross the street, she neglected to tell him not to climb ladders or attend birthday parties without being invited. You and your child will identify with Artie and his mom as they figure out what Artie "can do."

De Regniers, Beatrice Schenk
MAY I BRING A FRIEND?
Atheneum, 1964

A young boy is invited to tea with the King and Queen, but wants to bring a friend. He brings a giraffe and is naturally invited back for several other dining engagements. The young man returns each time with a new animal friend and as the story ends we find the King and Queen being feted for tea at the local zoo. A wonderful rhyme makes this a story that is easily memorized and read together.

---

*Doney, Meryl Illustrated by Gillian Gaze
THE VERY WORRIED SPARROW
Lion, 1978

Your child will identify with the very worried sparrow who finds reasons to worry about everything until he discovers the truth that "not one sparrow is forgotten by God." A well-told story with beautiful illustrations.

*Fisher, Leonard Everett
THE SEVEN DAYS OF CREATION
Holiday House, 1981

A stunning artistic interpretation of the Creation. The text is simple and Biblically accurate.

Flack, Marjorie
ANGUS AND THE DUCKS
Doubleday, 1930

Angus is a curious Scottie who manages to escape from the house to explore the world. His encounter with a flock of ducks will give you ample opportunity for sound effects and dramatic interpretation. His curiosity extends to cats *(Angus and the Cat)* and fellow dogs *(Angus and the Dog)* as well.

Freeman, Don
DANDELION
Viking Press, 1964

Dandelion the lion finds out his friends like him just the way he is. In fact they turn him away from a party because of his new outfit and permed mane. The theme is a familiar one in children's literature and Dandelion will be a favorite with your children. Freeman is a prolific author. Among the best titles are *Bearymore, A Pocket for Corduroy,* and *Norman the Doorman.*

Gramatky, Hardie
LITTLE TOOT
G.P. Putnam, 1939

The well-told tale of a little tugboat who has a hard time living up to the expectations of Father and Grandfather Toot. Other titles by the same author are: *Hercules, Loopy, Sparky, Little Toot on the Thames,* and *Little Toot on the Grand Canal.*

*Haubensak-Tellenbach, Margrit   Illustrated by Erna Emhardt
THE STORY OF NOAH'S ARK
Crown, 1977

A stunning artistic rendition of this favorite Bible story. The author takes liberties with the story, however, enhancing and expanding upon it.

**Ages
4-7**

Hoban, Russell   Illustrated by Lillian Hoban
BREAD AND JAM FOR FRANCES
Harper & Row, 1964

Frances is by far the most enchanting of all animal characters in children's literature. This badger will win your heart as she refuses to eat anything but bread and jam. Mother Badger uses a bit of clever psychology on Frances, and soon she is begging for more variety in her menu. Other titles are: *A Baby Sister for Frances, Bedtime for Frances, Best Friends for Frances, A Birthday for Frances*, and a new I Can Read Book, *A Bargain for Frances*.

Hutchins, Pat
DON'T FORGET THE BACON
Greenwillow, 1976

Although the text is simple, don't be fooled. The humor is much more sophisticated. Your five or six year old will delight as the main character tries to remember his mother's shopping list and ends up forgetting the bacon. I adore Pat Hutchins' stories, illustrations, and sense of humor. Although simple, her work is elegant. Other titles are: *The Wind Blew, Clocks and More Clocks, The Surprise Party*, and *Titch*.

*Keane, Glen
ADAM RACCOON IN LOST WOODS
David C. Cook, 1987

Adam Raccoon is an irrepressible animal with loads of personality. His journey with King Aren into the Lost Woods can be enjoyed on two levels—a delightful story with colorful cartoon illustrations and an allegory of the Christian life as we journey through the dark world. Other titles in the series are: *Adam Raccoon at Forever Falls* and *Adam Raccoon and the Circus Master*.

Keats, Ezra Jack
A LETTER TO AMY
Harper & Row, 1968

Ezra Jack Keats is famous for his collage illustrations. You will enjoy looking at the illustrations as well as reading about his young hero, Peter, who invites a neighborhood girl to his birthday party. Stories about Peter's other adventures can be found in *A Whistle for Willie, Peter's Chair,* and *The Snowy Day*.

Kellogg, Steven
THE MYSTERY OF THE MISSING RED MITTEN
Dial Press, 1974

If your child has ever lost a mitten, she will identify with Annie who has lost five this winter. You will explore many possibilities for where the mitten might be, before finding it used as the heart of a melting snowman. Kellogg is a wonderful author and illustrator with a gift for understanding the mind of a child. You will not go wrong with any of his stories: *The Mysterious Tadpole, Can I Keep Him?,* and *Much Bigger Than Martin*.

Kraus, Robert   Illustrated by Jose Aruego
WHOSE MOUSE ARE YOU?
Macmillan, 1970

Little Mouse is trying to figure out how he fits into his family. Although the text and pictures are simple, the concept is not. My children and I love both the illustrations and ideas in all of the Kraus books: *Leo the Late Bloomer* (for parents who wonder when their child will finally "bloom"), *Where Are You Going, Little Mouse?, Another Mouse to Feed,* and *Milton the Early Riser*.

Lionni, Leo
ALEXANDER AND THE WIND-UP MOUSE
Pantheon, 1969

You will want to read all of the Leo Lionni books aloud. Not only are the stories delightful, but Lionni's illustrations are works of art. Alexander the wind-up mouse is changed into a real mouse by a friend who wants to save his life. Look for these other Lionni books: *Inch by Inch, Swimmy,* and *Fish Is Fish.*

Ages 4-7

McCloskey, Robert
MAKE WAY FOR DUCKLINGS
Viking, 1941

You will no doubt remember this story from your own childhood. It tells how Mr. and Mrs. Mallard manage to raise their family of ducklings in the middle of Boston. Other McCloskey classics are *Blueberries for Sal, One Morning in Maine,* and *Lentil.*

*McKissack, Patricia C.   Illustrated by Bartholomew
LIGHTS OUT CHRISTOPHER
Augsburg, 1984

Christopher's red hair and freckles are definitely lovable. Reading about how he learns to cope with being afraid of the dark, telling the truth *(It's the Truth, Christopher),* or swearing *(Bad Mouth Christopher)* will help your child cope with the fears and problems that every child faces.

Marshall, James
GEORGE AND MARTHA
Houghton Mifflin, 1972

Each George and Martha book has five mini-stores about two engaging hippos. Animals who act like humans are a favorite source of material for children's authors and Marshall is especially skilled at creating vignettes that capture the relationship between good friends. Look for *George and Martha Encore, George and Martha Back in Town, George and Martha Tons of Fun, George and Martha One Fine Day,* and *George and Martha Rise and Shine.*

Milne, A.A.   Illustrated by E.H. Shepard
WINNIE-THE-POOH
E.P. Dutton, 1926

Winnie-the-Pooh is not strictly a picture book, since the illustrations are very small line drawings and the book numbers over 150 pages. However, the chapters are little stories and need not be read consecutively. Every child should know Christopher Robin, Winnie-the-Pooh, Eeyore, Little Roo, Rabbit, Owl, and Kanga. These are characters in children's literature with freshness and charm. Other titles by the author are: *The House at Pooh Corner, The World of Christopher Robin, The Pooh Song Book,* and *Pooh's Birthday Book.*

Rey, H.A.
CURIOUS GEORGE
Houghton Mifflin, 1941

Curious George probably entertained you when you were a child. There is something endearing about this curious monkey most likely associated with his ingenious ability to outwit almost every human he meets. Read all of the Curious George titles: *Curious George Takes a Job, Curious George Rides a Bike, Curious George Gets a Medal, Curious George Flies a Kite, Curious George Learns the Alphabet,* and *Curious George Goes to the Hospital.*

Seuss, Dr.
THE FIVE HUNDRED HATS OF BARTHOLOMEW CUBBINS
Vanguard Press, 1938

Dr. Seuss has two types of stories for children—easy to read, controlled vocabulary stories (See these under Books for the Independent Reader) and full length read alouds. Be prepared to read them over and over because children delight in the tongue twisters, imaginative rhymes, and alliteration. Suess' illustrations have never been among my favorites, but my children loved them. Some other Seuss favorites are: *And to Think That I Saw It on Mulberry Street, How the Grinch Stole Christmas, Horton Hatches the Egg, Horton Hears a Who, McElligot's Pool,* and *Yertle the Turtle.*

Slobodkina, Esphyr
CAPS FOR SALE
Addison Wesley, 1940

A timeless tale that children everywhere love to hear read aloud. This story of "a peddler, some monkeys, and their monkey business," is surprisingly fresh in its illustrations and text.

Ages 4-7

*Tangvald, Christine Harder   Illustrated by Gioia Fiammenghi
LEIF LIKES TO PLAY
David C. Cook, 1986

Leif is an irrepressible waif (My Friend Leif Series) who encounters the unlikely wherever he goes. He'll tickle your funny bone, while reminding you and your child to give thanks to God for the gifts of laughter and imagination. Other titles are: *Leif Needs a Bath, Leif Likes to Count,* and *Leif Cleans His Room.*

*Thigpen, Thomas Paul   Illustrated by Joyce John
COME SING GOD'S SONG
David C. Cook, 1987

This marvelous picture book is actually a six-verse song that celebrates God's glory from daybreak to nighttime. You can either "sing" or read the story since music is included. The illustrations are joyful and their mood matches the time of day. You'll have loads of fun with this one.

Turkle, Brinton
THY FRIEND, OBADIAH
Viking Press, 1969

Obadiah is an endearing six-year-old Quaker who lives in Colonial Nantucket. You'll get a flavor for life in a different historical period, but more importantly you'll read a well-told story. Other Obadiah titles are: *The Adventures of Obadiah, Obadiah the Bold,* and *Rachel and Obadiah.* Another wonderful Turkle book is *Deep in the Forest.* This wordless book can only be appreciated by the child who is acquainted with *Goldlilocks and the Three Bears* since it turns the tables and has a small bear as the uninvited guest in the home of a small girl and her parents.

Waber, Bernard
IRA SLEEPS OVER
Houghton, 1972

Ira can hardly wait to sleep over at his best friend's house. Naturally he plans to take along his teddy bear, until his sister ridicules his plan. When he discovers his friend Reggie's bear is called "Foo Foo," Ira returns home to get his own beloved "Tah Tah." Also by Bernard Waber: *Lyle, Lyle Crocodile; Lyle and the Birthday Party; The House on East 88th Street.*

Zion, Gene   Illustrated by Margaret Bloy Graham
HARRY THE DIRTY DOG
Harper & Row, 1956

Harry is a dog that everyone loves. His adventures are funny—but most importantly believable. Every child wishes that Harry could be their dog. Other titles include: *Harry By the Sea, No Roses for Harry,* and *Harry and the Lady Next Door.*

Zolotow, Charlotte   Illustrated by William Pene Du Bois
WILLIAM'S DOLL
Harper & Row, 1972

Charlotte Zolotow has collaborated with a variety of outstanding illustrators (Maurice Sendak, Garth Williams, Leonard Weisgard, and Kay Chorao) to create many wonderful picture books, each with a different style and type of story. The sentiments expressed in *William's Doll* should touch the heart of every father. William wants a doll and only his grandmother understands why that might be important. Other favorite Zolotow titles are: *Mr. Rabbit and the Lovely Present, Do You Know What I'll Do?, My Friend John, My Grandson Lew,* and *Hold My Hand.* There are over fifty Zolotow titles to choose from.

Books For The Independent Reader

The books in this category will serve two purposes—they can be read aloud to your child, but more importantly your child will eventually read them on his own. Books for the independent reader provide the beginning reader with well-written stories he can read on his own. This category of books has certain characteristics that make them unmistakable—small size, fairly large type, lots of white space, colorful illustrations on each page, and an easier to read, controlled vocabulary. Because of the shorter sentences and controlled vocabulary in these, be sure to include a wide variety of picture books also, so that your child can experience the richness of the English language.

Ages 4-7

Each publisher has its own imprint that signals an easy-to-read book. David C. Cook Publishing: I LOVE TO READ BOOK; Harper and Row: I CAN READ; Dial Press: A DIAL EASY-TO-READ-BOOK; Random House: PICTURE-BACKS, FIRST TIME BOOKS, BEGINNER BOOKS, and STEP INTO READING; Greenwillow Books: GREENWIL-LOW READ-ALONE; Coward-McCann, Inc.: A BREAK-OF-DAY BOOK; Scholastic: EASY TO READ FOLKTALES; and Platt & Munk: ALL ABOARD BOOKS. Look for these imprints when you are choosing books at the library or your bookstore for the beginning reader.

Benchley, Nathaniel   Illustrations by Arnold Lobel
SAM THE MINUTEMAN
(I Can Read History Book)
Harper & Row, 1969

If your child enjoys adventure stories with real people, Nathaniel Benchley provides them in his I CAN READ books. He brings the Revolutionary War to life in *Sam the Minuteman*. Other titles include *Oscar Otter, The Strange Disappearance of Arthur Cluck,* and *Red Fox and His Canoe.*

*Coleman, William Illustrated by Joan Artley Sterner
BERNIE SMITHWICK AND THE SUPER RED BALL
(I Love to Read Series)
David C. Cook, 1984

Bernie is a mischievous but lovable character who can't remember to mind his mother. His super red ball finds its way where it doesn't belong, and only by tying a string around his finger does Bernie solve his problem. Proverbs 6:20 takes on a new meaning: "Young man, obey your father and your mother. Tie their instructions around your finger so you won't forget." From the same author comes *Bernie Smithwick and the Purple Shoestring*, a charming tale of a missing purple shoestring.

Delton, Judy Illustrated by Giulio Maestro
TWO IS COMPANY
Crown, 1976

Although not designated an independent reader by the publisher, the story and reading level are perfect for the mid-second grader. Bear and Duck experience the familiar trauma of adding a third friend to their twosome. The author solves the problem in an unexpected way and the reader learns the true meaning of friendship. Another Bear and Duck Story is *Two Good Friends*.

Eastman, P.D.
GO, DOG, GO!
Random House, 1961

The covers of this book were taped together on more than one occasion at our house. The repetition of words and sentences will give your beginning reader confidence in his ability. Somehow a party of wild dogs on top of a tree will not seem too improbable after the fortieth or fiftieth reading of this favorite.

*Graeber, Charlotte Illustrated by Jack Stockman
UP, DOWN, AND AROUND THE RAIN TREE
(I Love to Read Series)
David C. Cook, 1984

The jungle provides a backdrop for a parrot, monkey, sloth, and puffbird to live and learn the simple lessons of living in harmony with friends and neighbors. *In, Out, and About Catfish Pond* is also part of the series. Both books give the beginning reader a good story with a well placed Christian emphasis.

**Ages
4-7**

Heilbroner, Joan Illustrated by P.D. Eastman
ROBERT THE ROSE HORSE
Random House, 1962

This book makes an appearance here because of my son Patrick. This story of a horse who is allergic to roses is an all-time favorite of his. Robert's story demonstrates that no matter what your talent, someone will come along who appreciates it.

Hoban, Lillian
ARTHUR'S PEN PAL
Harper & Row, 1976

Arthur and Violet are a charming brother-sister pair of chimpanzees that experience plenty of sibling rivalry along the way toward working out their problems together. The messages of loving, sharing, and caring come through loud and clear.

Hurd, Edith Thacher Illustrated by Clement Hurd
JOHNNY LION'S RUBBER BOOTS
(I Can Read Book)
Harper & Row, 1972

Any mother who has been stuck in the house on a rainy day with restless children will identify with Mother Lion as she attempts to keep Johnny amused. Fortunately Father Lion comes to the rescue with brand new rubber boots. *Johnny Lion's Book* is another favorite by the same author.

Lobel, Arnold
SMALL PIG
(I Can Read Book)
Harper & Row, 1969

This title numbers among the favorites of my children. Small Pig is an endearing character who leaves the farm because the farmer's wife has a penchant for cleanliness. Lobel is a master at writing simple but elegant stories. His *Frog and Toad* series is wonderful. You and your children will love the warm relationship between these two animals and identify with the experiences they have. Another favorite by Lobel is *Owl at Home*.

McKie, Roy and P.D. Eastman
SNOW
Random House, 1962

After reading this easy reader, you'll have to plan a snow picnic for your children.

*McKissack, Fredrick and Patricia   Illustrated by Joe Boddy
LOOK WHAT YOU'VE DONE NOW, MOSES
(I Love to Read Series)
David C. Cook, 1984

Here is a Bible story that early readers can handle with just a little help or all by themselves. Both you and your child will enjoy the "sound effect" words that accompany the plagues God sent to the Egyptians. Another title in the series is *Abram, Abram, Where Are We Going?*

Minarik, Elsa H.   Illustrated by Maurice Sendak
LITTLE BEAR'S VISIT
(I Can Read Book)
Harper & Row, 1961

Here is another I CAN READ series that is special! The gift of telling a beautiful story in a few and simple words has been bestowed on Elsa Minarik. Your children will be the benefactors of that gift. Other titles are *Little Bear, Father Bear Comes Home, Little Bear's Friend, Little Bear's Visit,* and *A Kiss for Little Bear.*

Parrish, Peggy   Illustrated by Wallace Tripp
COME BACK, AMELIA BEDELIA
(I Can Read Book)
Harper & Row, 1971

**Ages
4-7**

Amelia Bedelia is an intrepid housekeeper/nanny who takes everything literally. Children will delight as she follows all of her employer's instructions to the letter.

Seuss, Dr.
ONE FISH, TWO FISH, RED FISH, BLUE FISH
(Beginner Book)
Random House, 1960

No one has a way with words like Dr. Seuss. He puts them together in a rhyming fashion that captivates children. His drawings won't win any art awards, but kids don't care. They love the funny little children and weird looking animals. Children can read what he's written almost as easily as you can. There are dozens of titles but among the most popular are: *The Cat in the Hat, The Cat in the Hat Comes Back, Marvin K. Mooney, Will You Please Go Now, The Foot Book,* and *The Shape of Me and Other Stuff.* By Dr. Seuss under a different name (Theo. LeSieg) are: *In a People House, Hooper Humperdink? Not Him!,* and *Ten Apples Up on Top.*

Sharmat, Marjorie Weinman
NATE THE GREAT AND THE MISSING KEY
(A Break-of-day Book)
Coward, McCann, Inc., 1981

If your child enjoys solving a mystery, this series will challenge his thinking skills. Look for these other Nate the Great titles: *Nate the Great and the Fishy Prize, Nate the Great and the Lost List, Nate Goes Undercover, Nate the Great and the Phony Clue, Nate the Great and the Snowy Trail,* and *Nate the Great and the Sticky Case.*

Concept, Counting, And Alphabet Books For The Older Child

The books in this category are written for the older child. They demand a more sophisticated reader and teach more complex skills. They are an important source of continuing learning for your child.

Anno, Mitsumasa
ANNO'S COUNTING HOUSE
Philomel Books, 1982

This is the most sophisticated of the counting books. Two full pages of instructions are given. Through playing the games your child will be introduced to all sorts of advanced mathematical concepts. But most of all, she'll have a wonderful time seeing ten little people move from room to room in *Anno's Counting House.*

*Doney, Meryl
DISCOVERING SHAPES AND DESIGNS
Lion, 1980

Marvelous color photographs set forth the shapes and designs God has created in nature that have been duplicated by man. Christian non-fiction at its finest. Other titles in the series include *Discovering at the Zoo, Discovering Everyday Things, Discovering Colors, Discovering Out of Doors,* and *Discovering the City.*

Duvoisin, Roger
A FOR THE ARK
Lothrop, Lee & Shepard, 1952
More than a simple alphabet book, the complete story of Noah and the Ark is told. Your child will need a good attention span to complete all the letters of the alphabet as well as the matching game at the end of the book. You will learn some unusual animal names not encountered in many other read alouds.

Elting, Mary and Michael Folsom   Illustrated by Jack Kent
Q IS FOR DUCK
Clarion Books, 1980

This alphabet book calls for quick thinking. The reader has to figure out why A is for zoo, B is for dog, and C is for hen. The pictures are colorful and lively.

**Ages
4-7**

Emberley, Ed
ED EMBERLEY'S ABC
Little, Brown, 1978

Ed Emberley's distinctive style will tickle your funny bone while it helps your kindergarten or first grade child practice writing the letters of the alphabet. For each letter there is an animal doing something that results in another letter being formed. Typical of Emberley's sense of humor is the fact that not all of the letters come at the beginning of words.

Hoban, Russell   Illustrated by Sylvie Selig
TEN WHAT?
Charles Scribner, 1974

This counting book will be enjoyed by the older child because it solves a mystery. One urgent message and two secret agents take the reader off on a mysterious search.

Hoban, Tana
LOOK AGAIN?
Macmillan, 1971

Full page black and white photographs of nature's wonders can be viewed as a whole or in part through a small, cut out window. Readers have to sharpen their senses and figure out from the small segment just what the larger photograph contains. What seems like a game to your child is actually a very complex visual skill.

Kitchen, Bert
ANIMAL ALPHABET
Dial, 1986

This alphabet book is a work of art. The author has created stunning animal paintings that intertwine with full page block letters. The reader must guess the animal names, but for many you will need to consult the answer page found in the back of the book. Among the more unusual are quetzal, vulture, x-ray fish, and jerboa. This alphabet book is for the child interested in the unusual.

Spier, Peter
FAST-SLOW HIGH-LOW
Doubleday, 1972

To fully explore all of the opposites in this wordless book will take hours. Undoubtedly, your child will be willing to take every minute. Each opposite (over-under, young-old, and many others) has a full page of color illustrations which are often droll and whimsical. Plan to take several days exploring this book.

*Taylor, Kenneth Illustrated by Kathryn E. Shoemaker
BIG THOUGHTS FOR LITTLE PEOPLE
Tyndale, 1971

Although this is an ABC book, the alphabet definitely plays second fiddle to the lessons about Christian living that the author sets forth on a double-page spread. Each alphabet letter has a one-sentence rhyme, a paragraph explanation of the concept, some questions to answer, and a Bible verse that relates. The illustrations are beautifully done, and would stand alone very nicely with just the rhyme. A followup to this volume is *Giant Steps for Little People,* a similar format that explains The Sermon on the Mount and the Ten Commandments.

Folk And Fairy Tales

Folk and fairy tales continue to be an important source of literary challenge for the child. The most eminent Christian writers of fantasy like J.R.R. Tolkien and C. S. Lewis praised the fairy tale for its richness and ability to expand our thinking. Reading the familiar fairy tales to your children will exercise their imaginations and open limitless possibilities for creativity.

Ages 4-7

Brown, Marcia
STONE SOUP
Charles Scribner, 1975

Marcia Brown specializes in the interpretation of fairy tales and has won several Caldecott awards for her work. How do three hungry soldiers trick an entire village into donating vegetables and beef to make soup from a stone? Read this one aloud to find out. Other favorite fairy tales include: *Once a Mouse, Cinderella, Puss in Boots, Dick Whittington and His Cat,* and *The Steadfast Tin Soldier.*

Cauley, Lorinda Bryan
THE TOWN MOUSE AND THE COUNTRY MOUSE
G.P. Putnam, 1984

The age-old conflict between a simple life and one of rich and plenty is presented in this well-told tale. The finely laid table in a Victorian mansion is a visual delight. Other fairy tales by Cauley are: *Jack and the Beanstalk; The Cock, the Mouse, and the Little Red Hen; Goldilocks and the Three Bears.*

DePaola, Tomie
STREGA NONA
Prentice-Hall, 1975

This author has done extensive research into folktales, and his illustrations have an unmistakable charm. This Italian folktale centers around a magic pasta pot. Other DePaola titles are: *The Prince of the Dolomites* and *The Clown of God.*

Galdone, Paul
THE GINGERBREAD BOY
Clarion Books, 1975

Galdone does a masterful job of interpreting the best folk and fairy tales. His illustrations have a whimsy that brings new life to the stories. Sample them all! *The Little Red Hen, The Three Bears, The Three Billy Goats Gruff, The Magic Porridge Pot, Henny Penny, Little Tuppen,* and *Old Mother Hubbard and Her Dog* are among his many books.

Ginsburg, Mirra   Illustrated by Jose Aruego & Ariane Dewey
MUSHROOM IN THE RAIN
Macmillan, 1974

How can so many animals hide under one mushroom? The wise old frog explains—it's rain that makes the mushroom grow. This Russian folktale is wonderfully illustrated. Another folktale by Ginsburg is *Where Does the Sun Go At Night?*

Green, Norma   Illustrated by Eric Carle
THE HOLE IN THE DIKE
Thomas Y. Crowell, 1974

Green retells the story about the Dutch boy who holds his finger in the dike to save his village from flooding. Carle's illustrations are magnificent.

Hogrogian, Nonny
ONE FINE DAY
Macmillan, 1971

This American folktale is wonderful for reading aloud. A greedy fox learns that what he takes must be replaced.

Hyman, Trina Schart
LITTLE RED RIDING HOOD
Holiday House, 1983

Reviewers have called this artist's interpretation of the familiar fairy tales "romantic, lush, and mysterious." This retelling of Little Red Riding Hood has some humorous touches as well. As Little Red Riding Hood leaves Grandmother's house after barely escaping from her adventure with the wolf, she comforts herself with the thought that at least she minded her manners. Schart has illustrated other tales: *Snow White, The Sleeping Beauty,* and *Rapunzel.*

Ages 4-7

Jeffers, Susan
THUMBELINA
Dial Press, 1979

Susan Jeffers is a multi-talented artist whose interpretations of fairy tales and poetry are remarkable. Her illustrations add another element of appreciation to the familiar fairy tales. Look for these other titles: *Three Jovial Huntsman, Close Your Eyes,* and *Hansel and Gretel.*

Kellogg, Steven
PECOS BILL
William Morrow, 1986

I've never appreciated the Pecos Bill legend quite as much as I did when reading this re-telling by Kellogg. He has managed to bring all of the energy and excitement of a larger-than-life folk hero alive through his drawings.

Mosel, Arlene   Illustrated by Blair Lent
TIKKI, TIKKI, TEMBO
Holt, Rinehart & Winston, 1968

Legend has it that first and honored Chinese sons were always given very long names. This folktale tells how that custom was changed. Another folk tale by Mosel is *The Funny Little Woman.*

Oxenbury, Helen
THE HELEN OXENBURY NURSERY STORY BOOK
Alfred A. Knopf, 1985

A collection of the best-loved fairy tales with illustrations and translations suitable for the fours and fives.

*Scholey, Arthur   Illustrated by Ray and Corinne Burrows
BABOUSHKA
Crossway, 1982

This traditional Russian folktale has Baboushka traveling to Bethlethem to see the Christ-Child. She arrives too late, having tarried to prepare presents for the baby. Her search for the child goes on each Christmas when she leaves toys near sleeping children.

Tresselt, Alvin
THE MITTEN
Lothrop, Lee & Shepard, 1964

I've read this re-telling of a Ukranian folk-tale to hundreds of children over the years and never grow tired of it. Children are entranced by the idea of a mouse, frog, owl, rabbit, fox, wolf, boar, and bear settling in for the winter in a lost mitten. The illustrations are beautifully done.

Poetry
The poetry collections mentioned in chapter three will serve you very nicely as your children grow and mature. In addition, the following volumes are special.

Daniels, Mark Editor
A CHILD'S TREASURY OF POEMS
Dial, 1986

The classic poems are beautifully illustrated with over fifty full color paintings and black and white engravings from the Victorian and Edwardian era. A collector's item.

Ages 4-7

Hopkins, Lee Bennett Illustrated by Megan Lloyd
SURPRISES
Harper & Row, 1984

An I CAN READ poetry book collected by Lee Bennett Hopkins. This small volume is even indexed. Hooray!

O'Neill, Mary Illustrated by Leonard Weisgard
HAILSTONE AND HALIBUT BONES
Doubleday, 1961

An enduring volume that uses the colors as a basis for poems.

Prelutsky, Jack Illustrated by Robert Leydenfrost
A GOPHER IN THE GARDEN AND OTHER ANIMAL POEMS
Macmillan, 1967

Prelutsky's poems about animals are a challenge to read-aloud. You will find your tongue tangling if you're not careful.

5

The
Middle
Graders

Ages 8-10

I've never understood the parents who bemoan the passing of their children into the middle grades. To me, this period of time was the best of all possible worlds. My children were toilet trained and independent. But they weren't driving cars yet. Best of all they loved to talk about what they were reading.

Unable to keep up with the avalanche of new children's books that came tumbling into the school library where I worked, I tapped their expertise as book reviewers. We spent many evenings discussing just which books were good and why. Many of the suggestions that follow come from our experiences together as a family.

The years between eight and ten will find your child exploring a variety of social relationships. The children you will meet from this age group are concerned about friends, fitting in the group, and being accepted. They like to read about young people their own age meeting the challenges of growing up. Perhaps you'll recognize your own child among the group.

In the second part of the chapter you will find out which books are especially recommended for reading aloud to young people in this age category.

THE CHILDREN

Joe is eight years old. One of the most important people in his life right now is a new best friend, Mark. The two boys spend hours together making models or playing board games. The game of *LIFE* is a favorite. Joe is a collector of so many different things that his mother despairs of cleaning his room. Match-book covers, dinosaur models, comic books—nothing can ever be thrown away.

Joe is an excellent independent reader but still enjoys having his mother read aloud to him. His favorites so far are *Charlotte's Web* and *James and the Giant Peach*. His mom is an important person in his life and he is jealous of the time she spends on her work and with other family members. When they are home together, Joe follows her around the house asking questions and requiring her attention. She often feels as though she has a shadow.

Joe likes school and is eager to talk about what happens there with his family. When he was younger, getting him to share what went on in school was impossible. He also loves Sunday school. He is extremely interested in Bible stories, and is beginning to memorize short passages of Scripture. His membership in Awana Club is important to him, and he eagerly prepares for the memory assignments. He says his prayers with regularity each night and still wants a bedtime story.

The most tiresome aspect of Joe's personality at age eight is his readiness to engage in arguments and discussions. He is especially rude to his grandmother who lives with the family and is often sent to his room for losing his temper. But he never broods long over these temporary tempests and can rejoin the family group with no problem. He is usually willing to apologize, but often comes up with an excuse or alibi for his behavior. Joe is both a delight and challenge to his parents.

Samantha is nine years old and in fourth grade. She often comes forth with accurate descriptions and imitations of teachers and family friends. Her insights and outspokenness frequently embarrass her parents. She desperately wants to be thought of as "grown-up," and there are frequent arguments and disagreements over what kinds of clothing are most appropriate for a nine year old.

School is important to Samantha. She likes her teacher because she is fair, a quality that is extremely important to fourth-graders. Samantha's life is filled with activities from morning til night—reading, drawing, playing with her doll collection, practicing piano lessons, writing to Grandma, or just being with friends. She has a busy and well-organized social schedule.

Ages 8-10

Samantha is a willing helper to her mother, but needs frequent reminders to follow through on her jobs. She is often preoccupied with her own activities and doesn't bother to answer when called. This trait causes some friction between Mom and Samantha.

Samantha loves tales of make-believe and fantasy. Her favorite read-alouds are *Tales of the Kingdom* and the *Chronicles of Narnia*. Although she loves to read aloud to her younger brother and sister, she is beginning to prefer reading more difficult books on her own. She is an avid reader and won the One-Hundred Book Club award at school.

Part of her busy social schedule each week is attendance at Girl Scouts. Samantha is diligently earning badges and working on projects. Several girls from school attend with her and this makes going twice as much fun.

Samantha also is a regular user of the church library. She loves to read about girls who are slightly older and encountering all of the grown-up problems like boys and dates. Samantha is eagerly looking forward to growing up.

Dylan is ten years old, a most glorious age, according to his mother. He tinkers with old appliances around the house and last week reassembled a broken toaster with great success. He was able to help cook dinner when his mom had the flu. And only last week, his teacher called with an excellent report on what was happening in school.

Dylan is on the threshold of adolescence, and already his parents can see the young man he will become. His sensitive insight into people and their needs was evident when Dylan befriended a new boy in school that others were ridiculing. He takes the lessons he learns in Sunday school and family devotions very seriously and often reminds other members of his family of their responsibilities. Dylan loves to read about boys facing real-life danger with good triumphing over evil. One of his favorites is *In Search of Perlas Grandes*. He has many contemporary heroes in the sports world and is an avid football and baseball fan.

Dylan became a Christian during summer camp and is eager to read about real boys and girls encountering tests of their Christian faith in every day life. The D.J. Dillon Adventure Series is one of his favorites.

His best friend Matt lives just down the street, and they are inseparable. They frequently sleep over at each other's houses and exchange toys and comic books and work on school projects together. But Dylan still manages to find time to shoot baskets with his older brother. His parents are enjoying this period of relative calm in Dylan's life. They're using his interest and responsiveness to build a relationship that will carry them through the storms of adolescence.

THE CHOICES

The choices from which to make your read-aloud selections will be grouped in the following categories: Bible Storybooks and Bibles; Read-Aloud Novels; Poetry; Classics; Anthologies of Children's Literature; Legends, Myths, Folk and Fairy Tales. I've arranged the choices by author since many of our favorite authors have written several excellent read-alouds. Once you discover an author you like, there is great joy in reading all of his or her works. Christian books are indicated by an asterisk.

Bible Storybooks and Bibles

Some have suggested that Bible reading be looked upon as "dessert" after dinner in the evening. Becky Slough, a children's bookseller in Illinois, has set forth a number of excellent ideas for using the Bible as a read-aloud. She suggests that parents allow the Holy Spirit to be the primary instructive agent and concentrate on reading the passages in the best possible way with little comment.

I concur, having grown up in a home where dessert and the nightly Bible reading came together. There were never sermons or lectures, only the reading of the Word. We started at Genesis and read to Revelation. Only when we reached the Song of Solomon did we skip on to the next book. My father assured us that this book was better read silently.

Ages 8-10

The Bible can be read aloud to children on three levels: Bible storybooks, paraphrases, and translations. The Bible storybook retells the favorite Bible stories. The author brings his own interpretation to the retelling, and his choice of words dictates the complexity and level of sophistication. The paraphrase is a verse by verse rendition of the Bible in more contemporary language. The two most popular paraphrases—Phillips and the Living Bible—have been authored by individuals. The translation is the work of a group of scholars laboring over Hebrew and Greek texts, desiring to be quite exacting in their word-by-word translations. The Bible translation used in your church will most likely be the one you use with your family.

The following Bible storybooks and paraphrases are offered as a list from which you can choose your favorites. Get recommendations from your pastor or Christian education leaders. Visit your church library or Christian bookstore to preview as many titles as possible. Once you've selected a Bible storybook, a paraphrase, and a Bible translation to use in your family read-aloud sessions, you will want to make clear to your children the difference between them.

*Beers, V. Gilbert and Ronald A.
VICTOR FAMILY STORY BIBLE
Scripture Press, 1985

Although the illustrations vary in quality from story to story, the retellings of Bible stories are excellent. "Something to Think About" questions are included for each story.

*CHILDREN'S BIBLE
Golden Press, 1962

A long time favorite of many families, the stories are simply told and well illustrated.

*THE CHILDREN'S LIVING BIBLE
Tyndale, 1971

This is an ideal choice for a child's first Bible. Thirty-five full-color illustrations by Richard and Frances Hook are included. Other Tyndale publications featuring the Living Bible paraphrase are: *The Living Bible Storybook, The Young Reader's Large Print Edition, The Way* (a version specifically designed for young adults 14-24), and *The Book* (a special edition for the first time Bible reader including a more contemporary design and layout).

*Batchelor, Mary   Illustrated by John Haysom
THE CHILDREN'S BIBLE IN 365 STORIES
Lion, 1985

A finalist in the Gold Medallion Book Awards, this version has a read-aloud story for every day of the year. Illustrations are of the highest quality and the stories are well-written. Included are parts of the Bible not often covered in a Bible story anthology—Proverbs, Psalms, the Prophets, and New Testament letters.

*Hoth, Ira   Illustrated by Andre LeBlanc
PICTURE BIBLE
David C. Cook, 1978

The *Picture Bible* is perfect for those children who need more visual input to keep their interest in Bible stories. They will love the format that is similar to their familiar Sunday school papers. An excellent read-aloud activity could include taking turns reading the various captions.

*ILLUSTRATED BIBLE FOR CHILDREN
Nelson, 1973

Contains 185 paraphrased stories and is illustrated by Carlo Tora in full color.

**Ages
8-10**

*Roberts, Jenny   Illustrated by Alan Parry
LADYBIRD BIBLE STORYBOOK
Zondervan, 1983

Well-told stories with outstanding, detailed illustrations.

THE NEW TESTAMENT IN MODERN ENGLISH
J.B. Phillips   translator
Macmillan, 1972

A personal favorite of mine is this paraphrase. Although not as widely known as the *Living Bible,* this version is beautifully written and will be enjoyed when read aloud.

Read-Aloud Novels

Novels will be read over a longer period of time than shorter books. You may choose to read aloud a chapter per evening or read for extended periods while traveling. Titles fall into two primary categories: fantasy and realistic fiction. Expose your child to both categories. But, if you are encouraging your child to be an avid independent reader, concentrate on the type of stories she likes to hear and read. How dreadful to listen to hours of stories that do not excite, challenge, and engage you. Once you begin, your only difficulty will be in stopping your reading until the next read-aloud session. When your children begin borrowing the book to read ahead on their own, you will know that they are "hooked on books."

Alexander, Lloyd
THE BOOK OF THREE
Holt, Rinehart and Winston, 1964

The Chronicles of Prydain is a five-volume series of which this is the first. Based on Welsh mythology, they tell the story of Taran, the assistant pigkeeper, who with his band of companions defeats the forces of evil to become the High King. The five volumes tell a continuing story with each successive book written at a more difficult reading level: *The Black Cauldron, The Castle of Llyr, Taran Wanderer,* and *The High King.*

Brink, Carol Ryrie   Illustrated by Trina Schart Hyman
THE BAD TIMES OF IRMA BAUMLEIN
Macmillan, 1972

Irma Baumlein's first lie resulted in all sorts of terrible consequences—"like poisonous mushrooms out of a rotten log." This wonderful simile sets the stage for a realistic tale of just what can happen when you tell a "white lie." Brink writes just as eloquently about life in the Wisconsin frontier in the 1860s in *Caddie Woodlawn,* a Newbery Medal winner, as she does of modern life.

Burnett, Frances Hodgson   Illustrated by Tasha Tudor
THE SECRET GARDEN
J. B. Lippincott, 1911

This story enchanted me as a child. I became Mary Lenox, the willful orphan girl who enters the secret garden to discover her uncle's invalid child. Through her friendship with Colin, Mary experiences the true joy of giving to others. This is a challenging read-aloud; the language is descriptive and rich.

Burnford, Sheila
THE INCREDIBLE JOURNEY
Little, Brown, 1960

A frisky young Labrador retriever, an aging bull terrier, and a Siamese cat set out on a two-hundred-mile journey through a wooded wilderness to return to their home. The adventures encountered by this intrepid trio make wonderful fireside reading.

Ages 8-10

Butterworth, Oliver
THE ENORMOUS EGG
Little Brown, 1956; Dell, 1978

Twelve-year-old Nate Twitchell takes on the Washington establishment in an effort to save the dinosaur that hatched from "the enormous egg." The theme has amazing relevance thirty years after it was written.

Byars, Betsy
THE 18TH EMERGENCY
Viking, 1973

Nearly every middle-grade boy has been "picked on" by an older and bigger kid. Mouse is no exception. The difference is that he has asked for it. Marv Hamemerman is after him because of something Mouse wrote about him. The fear is palpable. The tension builds. Mouse finally faces Hammerman and takes his punishment in an honorable way. Middle graders love the books of Betsy Byars: *Goodbye Chicken Little, The House of Wings, The Summer of the Swans, Trouble River,* and *The Midnight Fox.*

Catling, Patrick Skene
CHOCOLATE TOUCH
William Morrow, 1979; Bantam, 1981

John Midas will remind your middle-grader of King Midas, whose touch turned everything to gold. John has a similar problem—everything he touches turns to chocolate. This story teaches a valuable lesson and reads aloud very well.

Cleary, Beverly
RAMONA THE PEST
Morrow, 1968; Dell, 1982

Life in the Quimby household is never dull when the younger of the Quimby children, Ramona, is on stage. This volume follows Ramona through her kindergarten year. Older readers will recall with delight their own experiences. This series is a good one to read to several children of different.ages. Other books in the series are: *Ramona and Her Father, Ramona the Brave, Ramona Quimby, Age Eight,* and *Ramona Forever.* Cleary has written some other excellent read-alouds like: *Dear Mr. Henshaw* and *The Mouse and the Motorcycle.*

Dahl, Roald   Illustrated by Nancy Ekholm Burkert
JAMES AND THE GIANT PEACH
Knopf, 1961; Bantam, 1978

Although Dahl has written many wonderful read-alouds, this one is my favorite. Dahl's gift is in making the ridiculous seem totally believable. The listener will immediately be caught up in this fantasy of a boy who flies away in a giant peach with a cast of incredible characters. Other Dahl classics are: *Charlie and the Chocolate Factory, Fantastic Mr. Fox,* and *Danny the Champion of the World.*

*Davis, Timothy C.
IN SEARCH OF PERLAS GRANDES
Accent Books, 1985

This is an exciting sea adventure that will have you eagerly looking forward to the next chapter. Fourteen-year-old Nathaniel Childe sets out in search of his father who is missing at sea. He is faced with making moral choices that challenge his beliefs. The Christian message is strongly communicated. Even though Nat lives in 18th century Boston, middle graders will have no problem relating to his struggles with integrity and loyalty.

Fitzgerald, John D.
THE GREAT BRAIN
Dial, 1967

**Ages
8-10**

This series is at the top of my son's list of favorites. The Great Brain is Tom Dennis. His brothers Sweyn and J. D. can scarcely keep up with the schemes he hatches. All of them make for hilarious reading. Every child would like to be a part of this family and can through the read-aloud experience. Other Great Brain books are: *More Adventures of the Great Brain, The Great Brain at the Academy, The Great Brain Does It Again, The Great Brain Reforms, Me and My Little Brain,* and *Return of The Great Brain.*

Fox, Paula
ONE-EYED CAT
Bradbury Press, 1984

The very moving story of a young boy who receives a rifle for Christmas from his uncle. Forbidden by his parents to touch it, he sneaks to the attic one night and uses it just once. Shooting at a shadow in the dark, he is uncertain about what he has hit. His uncertainty turns to guilt and fear when he sees a one-eyed wild cat prowling about his neighbor's yard. Certain that he has shot the cat's eye out, Ned's life is beset with guilt and fear. This book will touch anyone who has lived with unconfessed sin.

Godden, Rumer   Illustrated by William Pene DuBois
THE MOUSEWIFE
Viking, 1951

A gentle short story about a mouse who kindly frees a caged dove and in so doing sees the world in a new way. Other titles are: *Candy Floss, The Story of the Holly and the Ivy, Mouse House, The Fairy Doll,* and *Impunity Jane.*

Grahame, Kenneth   Illustrated by Michael Hague
THE WIND IN THE WILLOWS
Holt, Rinehart & Winston, 1980

There are dozens of versions of this timeless classic, but Michael Hague's illustrations make this one a collector's item. This book should definitely be read aloud! Children in the eight-to-ten age group who will most enjoy and appreciate the plot and humor are frequently unable to manage the vocabulary on their own. Don't worry about explaining the meanings of all of the words. Just read and let the context and flow of the story speak for itself.

Hale, Lucretia P.
THE COMPLETE PETERKIN PAPERS
Houghton Mifflin, 1960; Hale, 1981

The Peterkin family will amuse you with their bumbling attempts to handle everyday occurrences like snowstorms and salt in the coffee. There are dozens of vignettes of several pages each that relate their humorous attempts to solve problems together. Although set in the Victorian period, the Peterkins may remind you of your family from time to time. This 1960 edition is a reissue of all the Peterkin stories, some out of print since 1886.

---

*Hunkin, Oliver, editor   Illustrated by Alan Parry
DANGEROUS JOURNEY: THE STORY OF PILGRIM'S PROGRESS
Eerdmans, 1985

This edition of John Bunyan's *Pilgrim's Progress* is a collector's item for the superb illustrations alone. You will enjoy the selections that have been adapted, and the visual impact of the art will entrance you.

Juster, Norton
THE PHANTOM TOLLBOOTH
Random House, 1964

Be prepared for lots of challenging vocabulary and more than a few puns. In a kingdom of Dictionopolis, reigned over by King AZAZ the Unabridged, a young boy named Milo encounters unabridged fun. You may find yourself explaining many of the jokes to the less sophisticated reader, but this story is not to be missed.

**Ages
8-10**

Konigsburg, E. L.
**FROM THE MIXED UP FILES OF MRS. BASIL E.
FRANKWEILER**
Atheneum, 1978

Children will identify with Claudia and her younger brother Jamie, two big-city kids who run away from home to take up residence in the Metropolitan Museum of Art. There's nothing like a read-aloud to explore a different life-style. Once in the museum they are caught up in a mystery that adds suspense and excitement to the story. Konigsburg's other books are: *Jennifer, Hecate, Macbeth, William McKinley, and Me, Elizabeth; About the B'nai Bagels; Altogether, One at a Time; A Proud Taste for Scarlet and Miniver; The Dragon in the Ghetto Caper; The Second Mrs. Giaconda; Father's Arcane Daughter.*

Lawson, Robert
BEN AND ME
Little, Brown, 1939

A timeless favorite of middle-grade children. We find out that the real power behind Benjamin Franklin was a mouse named Amos. In this entertaining read-aloud, he tells just how he did it. Stories with similar themes are: *Mr. Revere and I* and *Captain Kidd's Cat.* Another good read-aloud by Lawson is *Rabbit Hill,* a Newbery Award winner in 1944.

*L'Engle, Madeleine
A WRINKLE IN TIME
Farrar, Straus & Giroux, 1962

Fantasy and science fiction that have Christian principles and allegory woven into their fabric best describes the work of Madeleine L'Engle. In the triumph of good over evil, Meg Murry and her younger brother Charles rescue their father from the great brain in the kingdom of Comazotz. Sequels are *The Wind in the Door* and *A Swiftly Tilting Planet*.

*Lewis, C. S.
THE LION, THE WITCH, AND THE WARDROBE
Macmillan, 1950

If you have limited time for reading aloud, let the Chronicles of Narnia be your very first choice. This is the first of a seven-book series written by a Cambridge professor who had no children of his own, but clearly understood the strong need of children for fantasy and magic. The Narnia series can be enjoyed on two levels—as a marvelously told tale of adventure and drama and as a Christian allegory that portrays the death and resurrection of Christ. The famous wardrobe that inspired these stories can be viewed at Wheaton College (Wheaton, Illinois) where many of Lewis' papers and letters have been collected.

Lindgren, Astrid
PIPPI LONGSTOCKING
Viking, 1950

The irrepressible Pippi Longstocking will shock and delight your children with her antics. Her mother has died and her father was lost at sea. Consequently she lives alone—which intrigues her two young next door neighbors. This read-aloud will intrigue your children as well. Other Pippi titles are *Pippi Goes on Board* and *Pippi in the South Seas*.

McCloskey, Robert
HOMER PRICE
Viking, 1943

Homer Price is the quintessential small-town boy and Centurburg's his town. Homer's most famous escapade involves a donut machine gone beserk. Looking for a diamond bracelet that slipped into the batter provides all the incentive people need to buy up Homer's inventory of donuts. *Centurburg Tales* related more of Homer's all-American antics.

*MacDonald, George   Illustrated by Linda Hill Griffith
THE PRINCESS AND THE GOBLIN
David C. Cook, 1985

Ages 8-10

This fantasy was written by the famed 19th century Scottish story-teller. MacDonald was revered by more contemporary writers of fantasy such as C.S. Lewis, J.R.R. Tolkien, and Charles Williams. Heroism blends with clear images of good and evil in a thrilling narrative of rescue. You will thrill as Princess Curdie is rescued from the mountain goblins. Also by the author: *The Christmas Stories of George MacDonald.*

MacLachlan, Patricia
SARAH, PLAIN AND TALL
Harper & Row, 1985

A moving story, beautifully told. I am deeply touched whenever I read this tale of a widower farmer with two children who advertises for a wife. Sarah, plain and tall, arrives, and although she misses the Maine seashore soon becomes mother to Caleb and Anna and wife to Papa. A Newbery winner.

*Mains, David and Karen   Illustrated by Jack Stockman
TALES OF THE KINGDOM
David C. Cook, 1983

This book was made to read aloud. Hero, the orphan boy, Princess

Amanda, and Dirty, the pig girl, are the characters conceived by the authors in this wonderful parable. A Christian fantasy that will move you deeply, *Tales of the Kingdom* is beautifully illustrated. This volume and its sequel, *Tales of the Resistance,* would make wonderful gifts for any child.

*Murphy, Elspeth Campbell   Illustrated by Tony Kenyon
MARY JO BENNETT
David C. Cook, 1985

Mary Jo Bennett is one of six kids in the Apple Street Church gang. *Danny Petrowski, Julie Chang, Pug McConnell, Becky Garcia,* and *Curtis Anderson* are the other kids. Each of them has recorded their secret thoughts in a prayer diary that lets us eavesdrop on what goes on in the mind of a primary grader. What a wonderful way to encourage children to write and talk to God on a daily basis.

O'Dell, Scott
ISLAND OF THE BLUE DOLPHINS
Houghton, 1960

This title won a Newbery Award in 1960 and was subsequently made into a film. A twelve-year-old Indian girl tries to save wild dogs that remain on the island from which her tribe has been removed. Her pluck and courage are inspiring to middle graders.

Paterson, Katherine
BRIDGE TO TERABITHIA
Thomas Y. Crowell, 1977

A Newbery Award winner, this story tells of the relationship between a ten-year-old boy, Jess, in rural Virginia and a newcomer to his town. Leslie, the newcomer, and Jess become fast friends and the tragedy of her death will touch you as it did him.

Peck, Robert Newton
SOUP
Knopf, 1974; Bantam, 1974

There has never been a pair of friends as delightful as Rob Peck and his best friend Soup. We know that Soup, otherwise known as Luther Wesley Vinson went on to become a minister, but when he and Rob Peck were growing up in a rural Vermont town in the 1920s, there was little mischief they didn't make. You will enjoy reading this series aloud just as must as your children will enjoy hearing it. These books are surefire winners for engaging boys who are reluctant readers. Other titles are: *Soup and Me, Soup for President, Soup on Wheels, Soup's Drum,* and *Soup's Goat.*

Ages 8-10

Rawls, Wilson
WHERE THE RED FERN GROWS
Doubleday, 1961; Bantam, 1974

Whenever this book is read aloud, you can be sure that tears will flow. The emotional impact of this story about a boy and his two dogs is a strong one. If you live with a child who has begged for a dog for his own or who deeply loves the dog he has, this story is must reading for you.

Robinson, Barbara
THE BEST CHRISTMAS PAGEANT EVER
Harper, 1972; Avon, 1973

If you've ever been in, directed, or watched a Sunday school Christmas program, this hilarious story will definitely be a favorite in your family. Imagine your Christmas program being taken over by a boorish bunch of kids who have absolutely no respect for anybody. Their total lack of understanding about the real meaning of the Christmas story only adds to the confusion. Make this a read-aloud tradition at your house every Christmas. You'll be reminded of what the holiday is really all about.

Rockwell, Thomas   Illustrated by Emily McCully
HOW TO EAT FRIED WORMS
Franklin Watts, 1973

You'll need a strong stomach to read this one aloud. In a bet designed to enlarge his savings account by fifty dollars, Billy Forrester assures his friends that he can eat fifteen worms. Amazingly enough, he wins!

*Roddy, Lee
THE HAIR-PULLING BEAR DOG
Scripture Press, 1985

Middle graders will enjoy listening to this adventure in the D.J. Dillon Adventure series. The author writes with authority about bear hunting in California's Sierra Nevada Mountains. An outstanding character in this story is Paul Stagg, a lay preacher. Through him, the author speaks convincingly of the need for Christ in D.J.'s life. Other titles in this well-written series are: *The City Bear's Adventures; Dooger, the Grasshopper Hound; The Ghost Dog of Stoney Ridge.*

Selden, George   Illustrated by Garth Williams
CRICKET IN TIMES SQUARE
Farrar, Straus & Giroux, 1960

The wonderful story of Chester Cricket, transported in a picnic basket from Connecticut to Times Square, New York. All of the characters in this read-aloud are enchanting and memorable—Harry the Cat, Tucker the Mouse, and of course Mario Bellini, the little boy who befriends and cares for Chester. I read this story to the first fifth-grade class I taught and have re-read it dozens of times, always with great success. A sequel to this is *Tucker's Countryside.*

Sharp, Margery
THE RESCUERS
Little, Brown, 1959

The rescuers in this charming tale are three mice, Miss Bianca, Bernard, and Nils. They have banded together as the Prisoners Aid Society and they undertake the rescue of a Norwegian poet from the Black Castle. Children can identify with the way in which tiny, powerless creatures like mice can cleverly accomplish worthy tasks. Some other titles are: *Miss Bianca in the Salt Mines, Miss Bianca,* and *Bernard the Brave: A Miss Bianca Story.*

**Ages
8-10**

*Tolkien, J.R.R.   Illustrated by Michael Hague
THE HOBBIT OR THERE AND BACK AGAIN
Houghton Mifflin, 1984

There are many versions of this classic, but this recently published one is wonderfully illustrated by Michael Hague and worth having. This is an ambitious read-aloud project, but one that will give you and your children much to think and talk about. If you enjoy fantasy with Christian allegory woven through, this read-aloud is for you. Bilbo Baggins is our hero and along with the wizard Gandalf and his band of dwarves, he faces all manner of dangers and terrors. *The Fellowship of the Ring, The Two Towers,* and *The Return of the King* comprise *The Lord of the Rings* trilogy and continue the story of the hobbits. The trilogy is more suitable for reading aloud to older children.

*Wangerin, Walter, Jr.   Illustrated by Daniel San Souci
POTTER
David C. Cook, 1985

Reality and fantasy are intertwined in this beautifully told tale of a young boy who experiences death and the resurrection as he travels through time and space. Never has the love of parents for a child been so eloquently portrayed as in this story. Wangerin has also written as poetic account of the creation called *In The Beginning There Was No Sky.*

White, E.B.   Illustrated by Garth Williams
CHARLOTTE'S WEB
Harper, 1952

This is one of our family's favorite read-alouds. White is such a fine writer that his story should be savored as fine chocolate. Adults will enjoy this tale as much or more than children. Charlotte is a gray spider who plans with Fern, the farmer's daughter, to save the life of Wilbur the pig. He is to be slaughtered, and the animals of the barnyard look to Charlotte to save him as she spins messages in her web proclaiming Wilbur's worth. Be prepared to shed tears at the conclusion of this story. White's other offerings for children are: *Stuart Little* and *The Trumpet of the Swan*.

Wilder, Laura Ingalls   Illustrated by Garth Williams
LITTLE HOUSE IN THE BIG WOODS
Harper & Row, 1953; 1971

The eight books in this series are a fictional account of the author's life in the late 19th century. Set in the middle west, there is ample opportunity for adventures galore. The remaining books in the series are: *Little House on the Prairie, Farmer Boy, On the Banks of Plum Creek, By the Shores of Silver Lake, The Long Winter, Little Town on the Prairie,* and *These Happy Golden Years*.

Poetry

The volumes recommended to you in chapters three and four will continue to be suitable for reading aloud at this age level since they contain a wide variety of poems. These additional volumes are especially chosen for the eight-to-ten age group.

Kennedy, X.J.
KNOCK AT A STAR
Little, Brown, 1982

In addition to being an excellent volume of poetry, this title is a teaching tool. Through small collections of poetry, the editor lets us know what poems do—make you laugh, tell stories, send messages, share feelings, and start you wondering. Other major sections include What's Inside a Poem, Special Kinds of Poetry, and Do It Yourself. This book is a must for the budding poetry writer.

Prelutsky, Jack   Illustrated by James Stevenson
THE NEW KID ON THE BLOCK
Greenwillow, 1984

Prelutsky is one of my favorites. His poems have wonderful humor and are eminently readable.

Silverstein, Shel
WHERE THE SIDEWALK ENDS
Harper & Row, 1974

Silverstein's wacky sense of humor and uninhibited observations on the world will delight even the most reluctant poetry reader. Kids are always checking this one out of the library. Be prepared for a little irreverence, however. Also by Silverstein: *The Light in the Attic.*

Classics

Classics are the books that you frequently attempted to read when you were young because your father said they were good for you. Often they held you spellbound. But just as frequently they were too difficult, and you failed to return to them when your reading skills improved. Reading the classics aloud to your children can expose them to a depth of vocabulary, thought, and creative expression seldom found in popular literature. But be selective. Read aloud only those books that truly interest you and your child. We have all of the following titles on our own book shelves since they were favorites in both my husband's and my childhoods. Sometimes we find they are assigned in school, and the children delight in being able to "check out" a book from our home library.

Since most of the titles will be published in a variety of editions, only author and titles will be listed.

Alcott, Louisa May
LITTLE WOMEN
LITTLE MEN
EIGHT COUSINS
ROSE IN BLOOM
JACK AND JILL
JO'S BOYS

Old-fashioned family stories. I adored them when I was growing up.

Burnett, Frances Hodgson
THE SECRET GARDEN

Look for a beautifully illustrated edition in Read-Aloud Novels.

---

*Bunyan, John
PILGRIM'S PROGRESS

Check out the edition earlier in the chapter for an outstanding read-aloud experience.

Carroll, Lewis
ALICE IN WONDERLAND
THROUGH THE LOOKING GLASS

This is my daughter's favorite. She loves fantasy and wacky humor. There are plenty of both in this classic. Look for the edition illustrated by Michael Hague for a lovely gift idea (Holt, Rinehart, Winston, 1985).

Defoe, Daniel
ROBINSON CRUSOE

This title was a favorite of my son's. All of us would like to think we have the survival instincts of Robinson Crusoe.

Dickens, Charles
A CHRISTMAS CAROL

A must for reading during the Christmas holidays.

**Ages
8-10**

Dodge, Mary Mapes
HANS BRINKER OR THE SILVER SKATES

If you live in a climate where ice skating is de rigeur, you'll enjoy this story. As part of my Dutch heritage, I'm very partial to it.

Grahame, Kenneth
THE WIND IN THE WILLOWS

Please read this one aloud to the whole family.

Irving, Washington
RIP VAN WINKLE

Challenging reading, but interesting.

Kipling, Rudyard
THE JUNGLE BOOK
JUST SO STORIES

These are both great read-alouds.

*MacDonald, George
THE PRINCESS AND THE GOBLIN
THE CHRISTMAS STORIES

The editions mentioned earlier in the chapter are worth having.

Rawlings, Marjorie Kinnan
THE YEARLING

A wonderful touching animal story. Please read it.

Spyri, Johanna
HEIDI

After you watch the movie, you'll have to read the book.

Stevenson, Robert Louis
TREASURE ISLAND
KIDNAPPED

Exciting adventure for both boys and girls. Good reading after viewing the movie classics.

Twain, Mark
A CONNECTICUT YANKEE IN KING ARTHUR'S COURT
THE ADVENTURES OF TOM SAWYER
THE ADVENTURES OF HUCKLEBERRY FINN
THE PRINCE AND THE PAUPER

These are more sophisticated reading. Use your own judgement for your family. They are frequently assigned in junior high and high school literature classes.

Anthologies Of Children's Literature

An anthology contains a collection of different stories that is handy to have available for read-aloud sessions. The collection gives you a variety of different selections all in one easy location.

Fadiman, Clifton
THE WORLD TREASURY OF CHILDREN'S LITERATURE
Little, Brown, 1984, 1985

Martignoni, Margaret
THE ILLUSTRATED TREASURY OF CHILDREN'S LITERATURE
Grossett & Dunlap, 1955

Russell, William F.
CLASSICS TO READ ALOUD TO YOUR CHILDREN
Crown Publishers, 1984

Ages 8-10

Untermeyer, Louis
THE GOLDEN TREASURY OF CHILDREN'S LITERATURE
Golden, 1985

Legends, Myths, Folk and Fairy Tales

There are hundreds of wonderful retellings of folk and fairy tales complete with illustrations that are perfect for reading aloud to younger children (see chapter four). However, if you wish to pursue folk and fairy tales in more depth, you will want complete anthologies. My daughter and I have collected the following anthologies over the years, and they make wonderful read-alouds.

Alderson, Brian, translator   Illustrated by Michael Foreman
THE BROTHERS GRIMM: POPULAR FOLK TALES
Doubleday, 1976

Briggs, Raymond, illustrator
THE FAIRY TALE TREASURY
Coward, McCann & Geoghegan, 1972

Foreman, Michael, illustrator
HANS CHRISTIAN ANDERSEN, HIS CLASSIC FAIRY TALES
Doubleday, 1974

Hague, Michael, illustrator
MICHAEL HAGUE'S FAVORITE HANS CHRISTIAN ANDERSEN FAIRY TALES
Holt, Rinehart, Winston, 1981

Harris, Joel Chandler
COMPLETE TALES OF UNCLE REMUS
Houghton Mifflin, 1955

Haugard, Erik Christian, translator
HANS CHRISTIAN ANDERSEN: THE COMPLETE FAIRY TALES AND STORIES
Doubleday, 1974

Holden, Heidi
AESOP'S FABLES
Viking Press, 1981

Manheim, Ralph, translator
GRIMM'S TALES FOR YOUNG AND OLD
Doubleday, 1971

Manheim, Ralph, translator   Illustrated by Erick Blegvad
RARE TREASURES FROM GRIMM
Doubleday, 1981

Mayer, Marianna   Illustrated by Gerald McDermott
ALADDIN AND THE ENCHANTED LAMP
Macmillan, 1985

Nielsen, Kay, illustrator
FAIRY TALES BY HANS CHRISTIAN ANDERSEN
Viking Press, 1981

O'Brien, Edna   Illustrated by Michael Foreman
TALES FOR THE TELLING: IRISH FOLK AND FAIRY TALES
Atheneum, 1986

Ages 8-10

Price, Margaret Evans
MYTHS AND ENCHANTMENT TALES
Rand McNally, 1924

Segal, Lore, translator   Illustrated by Maurice Sendak
THE JUNIPER TREE AND OTHER TALES FROM GRIMM
Farrar, Straus & Giroux, 1973

Singer, Isaac Bashevis
STORIES FOR CHILDREN
Farrar, Straus & Giroux, 1984

6

Books To Entice The Reluctant Reader

Ages 10-12

Teachers frequently assign book reports to students in their classes. More often than not, they let students choose what they want to read. As a school librarian, I was often faced with the task of helping Stuart find a book. Stuart was a reluctant reader. He would wander through the library with his hands in his pockets trying to look busy. But the astute observer could tell that Stuart was simply not interested in choosing a book.

The trick to helping children like Stuart choose books is to find a book that catches their interest and then to have several more like it, ready to thrust into their hands when they've finished the first. The book needs to be fairly easy-to-read, have a predictable plot, and have characters to whom children can easily relate. I often hooked children like Stuart on books by introducing them to Encyclopedia Brown, a young detective. Readers try to outsmart the author and have a chance to check on their sleuthing powers by comparing their solution to the author's.

Did you ever get hooked on a series of books like the Sugar Creek Gang, Bobbsey Twins, Nancy Drew, or the Hardy Boys? They certainly don't qualify as great literature, but they meet a need that many children have for repetition and predictability. The recommendations in this category will not necessarily stand the read-aloud test, but they will usually 127 entice a reluctant reader who is uneasy with complicated plots, difficult vocabulary, and unusual characters and settings. Of course the recommendations in this chapter aren't just for reluctant readers. Good readers will enjoy these stories also! Don't be afraid to sample a variety of series until you find just the right one for your reluctant reader. Each series has its own unique characters and setting. Availability of the books in either hardback or paperback will also be indicated.

The books in this category are most appropriate for children between the ages of ten and twelve, although there is certainly leeway on either end of the age guidelines depending on interest and reading ability. Christian series are indicated with an asterisk.

*Ashley, Meg
BOARDING HOUSE ADVENTURE SERIES
Regal Books (paperback)

Action packed mysteries. Titles include: *Secret of the Old House, The Deserted Rooms, Lights in the Lake,* and *Danger on the Quarry Path.*

*Bly, Stephen and Janet
CRYSTAL BLAKE BOOKS
David C. Cook (paperback)

Crystal is fourteen and new to the Idaho mountains. How she copes with being the new kid in town is the focus of this series. Titles are: *Crystal's Perilous Ride, Crystal's Solid Gold Discovery, Crystal's Rodeo Debut, Crystal's Mill Town Mystery, Crystal's Blizzard Trek,* and *Crystal's Grand Entry.*

Cleary, Beverly
RAMONA BOOKS
HENRY BOOKS
Morrow (hardcover); Dell (paperback)

Although this author was included in the read-aloud section, her inclusion here is also appropriate. She is an immensely popular author with children and they usually get hooked on the Cleary books and read non-stop through all of them: *Ramona and Her Father, Ramona the Brave, Ramona Quimby, Age Eight, Ramona Forever, Ramona the Pest, Beezus and Ramona.* Another very popular Cleary series revolves around an engaging young man named Henry. Titles are: *Henry Huggins, Henry and Ribsy, Henry and the Paper Route, Henry and the Clubhouse,* and *Henry and Beezus.*

CHOOSE YOUR OWN ADVENTURES SERIES
Bantam (paperback)

Ages 10-12

The books in this series are never read straight through—a concept that really appeals to kids. Instead, the reader makes choices based on how he thinks the story will unfold. For example—if you decide it would be wiser to stay hidden in the cave, you turn to page 4. If you're adventuresome and want to set out through the tunnel, you turn to page 7. Many authors have contributed to the series. The titles come individually or in boxed sets.

*Clifford, Laurie B.
PEPPERMINT GANG SERIES
Tyndale (paperback)

The Peppermint Gang live together on a mission compound. This is an adventure series that will appeal to both boys and girls. Titles include: *The Peppermint Gang and the Evergreen Castle, The Peppermint Gang and the Secret Golden Crosses, The Peppermint Gang and the Million Dollar Night,* and *The Peppermint Gang and Frog Heaven.*

*Courtney, Dayle
THORNE TWINS ADVENTURE BOOKS
Standard (paperback)

In the same genre as Hardy Boys and Nancy Drew, these mysteries will find your reluctant reader coming back for more. These books have particularly intriguing titles. The choices include: *Flight to Terror, Escape from Eden, Knife with Eyes, The Ivy Plot, Operation Doomsday, Omen of the Flying Light, Three-ring Inferno, Mysterious Strangers, The Foxworth Hunt, Jaws of Terror, The Hidden Cave, Tower of Flames, The Trail of Bigfoot, Shadow of Fear, The House That Ate People,* and *The Sinister Circle.*

Hicks, Clifford B.   Illustrated by Bill Sokol
ALVIN FERNALD SERIES
Holt, Rinehart, & Winston (hardback)

Alvin is a likeable young man who gets involved in solving mysteries in the pleasant little Iowa town of Riverton. Titles in the series are: *Alvin's Swap Shop; Alvin Fernald, Superweasel; Alvin Fernald, Mayor for a Day; Alvin Fernald, Foreign Trader; Alvin's Secret Code; The Marvelous Inventions of Alvin Fernald.*

---

*Hutchens, Paul
SUGAR CREEK GANG SERIES
Moody Press (paperback)

This enduring adventure series is over forty years old and still going strong. I loved it when I was growing up. Titles include: *The Killer Bear, The Winter Rescue, The Lost Campers,* and *The Secret Hideout.* If you have the money and time, you can purchase and read over thirty Sugar Creek Gang books.

---

*Jenkins, Jerry B.
THE BRADFORD FAMILY ADVENTURES
Standard (paperback)

The Bradford family might be like yours, and therein lies its attraction for reluctant readers. Titles in the series are: *Daniel's Big Surprise, Two Runaways, The Kidnapping, Blizzard, 14 Days to Midnight, Good Sport, Bad Sport, The Clubhouse Mystery,* and *Marty's Secret*

*Jenkins, Jerry B.
DALLAS O'NEIL AND THE BAKER STREET SPORTS CLUB
Moody Press (paperback)

There are eight titles in this series and they cover nearly all the sports your child might play: *The Secret Baseball Challenge, The Scary Basketball Player, The Mysterious Football Team, The Weird Soccer Match, The Strange Swimming Coach, The Bizarre Hockey Tournament, The Silent Track Star,* and *The Angry Gymnast.*

Ages 10-12

*Johnson, Ruth I.
JOY SPARTON SERIES
Moody Press (paperback)

A contemporary series with a definite Christian emphasis, the stories tell of two preacher's kids growing up. Titles include: *Joy Sparton of Parsonage Hill, Joy Sparton and the Vacation Mix-Up, Joy Sparton and the Money Mix-Up, Joy Sparton and the Problem Twin,* and *Joy Sparton and the Mystery in Room Seven.*

*Leppard, Lois Gladys
A MANDIE BOOK
Bethany House Publishers (paperback)

This series tells stories about Mandie, a turn-of-the-century preteen in North Carolina. Titles are: *Mandie and the Secret Tunnel, Mandie and the Cherokee Legend, Mandie and the Ghost Bandits, Mandie and the Forbidden Attic, Mandie and the Trunk's Secret, Mandie and the Medicine Man,* and *Mandie and the Charleston Phantom.*

*Lutz, Norma Jean
MARCIA STALLINGS SERIES
David C. Cook (paperback)

Marcia, age 13, moves from an Oklahoma ranch to the city. In addition she acquires a new mother. Titles are: *Good-bye Beedee, Once Over Lightly,* and *Oklahoma Summer.*

MacGregor, Ellen and Dora Pantell   Illustrated by Charles Geer
MISS PICKERELL SERIES
McGraw Hill (hardback)

Miss Pickerell is an intrepid adventurer who will take on any challenge. Titles in the series are: *Miss Pickerell Goes to Mars, Miss Pickerell and the Geiger Counter, Miss Pickerell Goes Undersea, Miss Pickerell Goes to the Arctic, Miss Pickerell on the Moon, Miss Pickerell Goes on a Dig, Miss Pickerell Harvests the Sea, Miss Pickerell and the Weather Satellite, Miss Pickerell Meets Mr. H.U.M.,* and *Miss Pickerell Takes the Bull By the Horns.*

*MAKING CHOICES BOOKS
David C. Cook (paperback)

The Christian counterpart to the Choose Your Own Adventure Series, this series gives young people an opportunity to practice Christian decision making while enjoying an adventure story. Titles are: *Help! I'm Shrinking!, Avalanche!, The Hawaiian Computer Mystery, Help! I'm Drowning, Mr. X's Golden Scheme, Trouble in Quartz Mountain Tunnel, A Horse Named Funny Bits, The Cereal Box Adventures, Dr. Zarnof's Evil Plot, Flight Into the Unknown, President's Stuck in the Mud, Professor Q's Mysterious Machine, Dog Food and Other Delights,* and *General K's Victory Tour.*

*Nielsen, Shelly
VICTORIA MAHONEY SERIES
David C. Cook (paperback)

Victoria is a preteen who goes through the usual traumas of junior high while learning about faith, friendship, and growing up. Titles include: *Just Victoria, More Victoria, Take a Bow, Victoria,* and *Only Kidding, Victoria.*

*PENNYPINCHER SERIES
David C. Cook (paperback)

This series is comprised of a wide variety of titles and authors. Each is geared to the preteen or young teen reader and focuses on youthful problems. Some of the best titles are: *All Alone Except for My Dog Friday, Batting Ninth for the Braves, A Horse Named Cinnamon, The Treasure of the Scroll, Secret of the Painted Idol, The Claw and the Spiderweb, The Year I Went to High School with My Parents, To Catch a Golden Ring, Brad Benson and the Secret Weapon,* and *42 Red on Four.*

Ages 10-12

*Richardson, Arleta
GRANDMA'S ATTIC SERIES
David C. Cook, (paperback)

Nostalgia for times when Grandma (possibly Great-Grandma) was a girl will entice your reluctant reader into this series. Titles are: *In Grandma's Attic, More Stories from Grandma's Attic, Still More Stories from Grandma's Attic, Treasures from Grandma, Sixteen and Away from Home, Eighteen and On Her Own,* and *Nineteen and Wedding Bells Ahead.*

Robertson, Keith
HENRY REED SERIES
Viking (hardcover)

The Henry Reed series isn't as easy-to-read as some of the other series, but the interest level is extremely high. Henry gets older as the series progresses, but in the beginning stories he is thirteen. He is one of the most likeable young men in children's literature. In the journal he keeps which comprise the books, you'll join him in his business enterprises. Titles are: *Henry Reed, Inc., Henry Reed's Baby-Sitting Service, Henry Reed's Big Show, Henry Reed's Journey,* and *Henry Reed's Think Tank.*

*Roddy, Lee
D.J. DILLON SERIES
Scripture Press (paperback)

Lots of exciting animal adventures set in the Sierra Nevada mountains by the author of "Grizzly Adams." Titles are: *D.J. Dillon and the City Bear's Adventures, D.J. Dillon and Dooger, The Grasshopper Hound, D.J. Dillon and the Ghost Dog of Stoney Ridge,* and *D.J. Dillon and the Hair-pulling Bear Dog.*

Sobol, Donald J.   Illustrated by Leonard Shortall
ENCYCLOPEDIA BROWN
E.P. Dutton (hardcover); Bantam (paperback)

Readers can work at solving the mysteries along with boy detective, Encyclopedia Brown. Solutions for each ten-to-twelve-page mystery can be found in the back of the book. Each volume contains ten mysteries. Some of the many titles are: *Encyclopedia Brown Keeps the Peace, Encyclopedia Brown Gets His Man, Encyclopedia Brown Finds the Clues, Encyclopedia Brown and the Case of the Secret Pitch,* and *Encyclopedia Brown, Boy Detective.*

*Smith, Bonnie Sours
THE DORRIE BOOKS
David C. Cook (paperback)

Dorrie is a homeless girl, and the series tells of how faith in God helps her growing up in her aunt's home. Titles are: *If You Love Me, Call Me Dorrie, Dorrie and the Mystery of Angell Swamp,* and *A Dream for Dorrie.*

*Sommer, Karen
THE SATCH BOOKS
David C. Cook (paperback)

Satch finds out that growing up isn't always easy. This series provides a humorous approach to the stresses in a boy's life. Titles in the series are: *Satch and the New Kid* and *Satch and the Motormouth.*

*Sorenson, Jane
JENNIFER BOOKS
Standard (paperback)

Jennifer and her family are a typical American family, and Jennifer has her share of adolescent crises. Titles in the series are: *It's Me, Jennifer, It's Your Move, Jennifer, Jennifer Says Good-bye, Jennifer's New Life, Boy Friend, Once Upon a Friendship, Fifteen Hands,* and *In Another Land.*

*Stahl, Hilda
ELIZABETH GAIL SERIES
Tyndale (paperback)

Elizabeth Gail Dobbs is a foster child, and this series tells about how she grows up and copes with the loss of her family. There are eighteen books in the series—among them: *Elizabeth Gail and the Mystery at the Johnson Farm, E.G. and the Secret Box, E.G. and the Teddy Bear Mystery,* and *E.G. and the Dangerous Double.* Stahl has also written two other series published by Tyndale: The TINA SERIES and the TEDDY JO SERIES.

Ages 10-12

Warner, Gertrude Chandler
ALDEN FAMILY MYSTERIES
Albert Whitman & Company (hardback)

I read my first Warner mystery in third or fourth grade and then proceeded to read the entire series. Your child will enjoy all of these titles: *The Boxcar Children, Surprise Island, The Yellow House Mystery, Mystery Ranch, Mike's Mystery, Blue Bay Mystery, The Woodshed Mystery, The Lighthouse Mystery, Mountain Top Mystery, Schoolhouse Mystery, Caboose Mystery, Houseboat Mystery, Snowbound Mystery, Tree House Mystery, Bicycle Mystery, Mystery in the Sand, Mystery Behind the Wall,* and *Bus Station Mystery.*

Williams, Jay and Raymond Abrashkin
Illustrated by Owen Kampen
DANNY DUNN SERIES
McGraw Hill (hardback) Archway (paperback)

Danny Dunn and his friend Professor Bullfinch are always involved in some wacky new scheme or invention. Among the titles in the series are: *Danny Dunn and the Automatic House, Danny Dunn and the Anti-Gravity Paint, Danny Dunn on a Desert Island, Danny Dunn and the Homework Machine, Danny Dunn and the Weather Machine, Danny Dunn on the Ocean Floor, Danny Dunn and the Fossil Cave, Danny Dunn and the Heat Ray,* and *Danny Dunn, Time Traveler.*

7

Rate Your School's Reading Quotient

When I was a librarian in a suburban elementary school, I campaigned for the adoption of a practice called Sustained Silent Reading (SSR). How could children, I argued to my fellow faculty members, gain fluency and ease in their reading if they didn't practice? I didn't count the time they spent filling in blanks or drawing lines to correct answers as *reading*. To me, reading meant being curled up with a good book while the rest of the world went by.

And further, I argued, how could children learn the true value of reading if they had no adult role models. Children want to do what they see grown-ups doing. Sustained Silent Reading calls for students to read silently in class for a prescribed period. In addition, the teacher must read silently with the students.

All the teachers but one were willing to cooperate. She was dubious about spending her valuable time reading in the classroom. "I don't like to read," she protested. "Why can't I grade papers instead?"

"You've totally missed the point," I told her, trying to keep my rising impatience under control. "You've got to demonstrate to your students that reading is such a worthwhile activity that you'll even postpone grading papers to do it yourself."

"OK," she agreed. "But what will I read? I don't like

to read." I thought about all of the reluctant readers I had tempted over the years with *Charlie and the Chocolate Factory* or *Charlotte's Web.* I would have to come up with something just a bit different for this middle-aged reader, so I suggested a paperback romance.

Before I knew it SSR was going full steam in her classroom. I could almost have predicted what happened next. The teacher wasn't just reading during Sustained Silent Reading. She was reading during lunchtime in the teachers' lounge. When she was nearly finished with the 300-page novel, she asked for another recommendation.

My story has two points. First, it's never too late to get "hooked" on books. But second, and more important, children need to have role models who demonstrate on a daily basis that reading is enjoyable and important. Teachers, principals, and other school personnel need to recognize the importance of reading and then develop and implement outstanding reading programs. When parents find excellent programs they need to applaud and encourage them.

But what should you do if you aren't satisfied with your school's reading program? What should the role of the Christian parent be with regard to evaluating and effecting change in schools, both Christian and public? Our responsibilities as Christian parents dictate none other than a high profile role. When you are tempted to leave the involvement and the effecting change to others, remember these admonitions from the Gospel of Matthew: "You are the world's seasoning, to make it tolerable. . . . You are the world's light—a city on a hill glowing in the night for all to see. Don't hide your light! Let it shine for all; let your good deeds glow for all to see."

As a parent, you have every reason to expect that the school your child attends, whether Christian or public, will do a good job of teaching reading, will emphasize the importance of reading, and will provide many opportunities for your child to practice reading skills. Perhaps you are uneasy about what you see happening in your school but aren't certain just where to begin.

How can you evaluate whether your school has a good reading program? The following checklist should give you a start as you talk to the principal and teachers, observe in the classroom, and become familiar with the kinds of experiences your child is having at school. As you find answers to the following questions you will be able to rate your school's RQ (Reading Quotient).

READING QUOTIENT CHECKLIST

There are ten items in the Reading Quotient Checklist and the following scoring guide will help you decide how your school rates:

SUPERIOR READING QUOTIENT: Nine or ten of the following characteristics describe your school, its staff, and reading program.

EXCELLENT READING QUOTIENT: Seven or eight of the following characteristics describe your school, its staff, and reading program.

GOOD READING READING QUOTIENT: Five or six of the following characteristics describe your school, its staff, and reading program.

POOR READING QUOTIENT: Less than five of the following characteristics indicates that changes are needed in your school's reading program.

The characteristics are listed in their order of importance with the first seven being critical.

1. Does your school have an organized reading curriculum with stated learner outcomes for each grade level?

Teachers need an organized curriculum on which to base their reading instruction. Diagnostic and criterion tests usually accompany the curriculum to help the teacher determine if students have mastered the skills.

2. Does the principal talk knowledgeably about the school's reading instruction program?

One of the key components that contributes to the quality of a school is its principal. Teachers respond to the expectations of the principal. If your principal expects quality reading instruction and emphasizes its importance, there is a strong likelihood that a good program will exist.

3. Does the beginning reading program contain a well organized and comprehensive phonics program?

All students can benefit from a comprehensive phonics program to teach the letter/sound relationships. Through a phonics program they will be able to sound out words on their own and get off to a good start in both reading and spelling. Ask teachers or the principal if phonics is included in the program.

4. If children are grouped for reading, does the possibility of moving from one instructional group to another exist?

Students who are having difficulty may need to repeat instruction in a certain skill. On the other hand, the student who takes a sudden spurt in reading ability should never be held back because of grouping.

5. Does the reading program emphasize the real purpose of reading—meaning/comprehension?

The teachers should never equate reading with filling in spaces on workbook pages. The emphasis should always be on comprehension of what is read.

6. Does each classroom have a variety of materials available for students to read during free time?

The good teacher always has a collection of interesting books and magazines that students can pick up when they have finished their work and have time for free reading.

7. Does the school offer remedial programs for those students who are having problems? And conversely, are there enrichment or acceleration programs for students who are superior readers?

Your school should carefully monitor every student and intervene with special help if a student is having difficulty learning to read or is capable of moving more quickly. This intervention should occur as early as possible in a child's schooling.

8. Is there a library or resource center to provide a rich and varied sampling of library books for recreational reading?

Reading instruction should never be limited to just the "reading book." Students should be encouraged and often required to read all kinds of books. A weekly library period should be provided for story hours and regular check-out of books.

9. Does the school welcome parents as volunteers in its classrooms and library?

The effective school utilizes parent resources to work with students who may be having problems.

10. Are there school-wide programs that offer incentives to students for independent reading?

Does the library have a book club or discussion group for students who read independently? Are there contests that give prizes for independent reading? Is there a school-wide Sustained Silent Reading Program?

ACTION PLAN FOR SCHOOL IMPROVEMENT

The evaluation of any program should always be undertaken from a positive perspective. No school will be perfect. There will always be room for improvement and enhancement. Here is where the "light" and "salt" that we spoke of earlier can begin to shine and flavor. Your involvement can come at many levels depending on your time and talents.

The following suggestions for what you can do to improve the reading program in your child's school are listed according to the level of involvement needed. You can be a silent prayer partner or you can be a highly visible school board member.

1. Pray regularly for the teachers and principal of your child's school. Ask for God's wisdom and guidance for them

as they work daily at a very challenging task—teaching and guiding children.

2. Make an appointment to see your child's teacher and principal and talk about the questions given in the Reading Quotient Checklist. Become knowledgeable about what is happening in your child's school. Undertake this project as a *learner.*

3. Volunteer as a classroom or library assistant. You can read stories to classes, tutor an individual student, work with groups of students on puppet shows or plays, or give book talks.

4. Invite speakers to PTA meetings who are knowledgeable about reading instruction.

5. Work to raise funds through the PTA to purchase books for the school library.

6. Organize a Birthday Book program at your school where parents purchase a book for the school library on their child's birthday.

7. Offer to organize a school-wide reading incentive program. Run a reading contest in which students fill out tickets for each hour of reading time. Deposit the tickets in a barrel and draw for prizes. Local merchants could donate prizes or you could award tickets to an athletic event.

8. Establish a paperback book exchange staffed by PTA members. Students turn in their old paperbacks and are given credits to select others in exchange.

9. Organize a course for parents through the local high school adult education program. The course could focus on introducing parents to the reading process and suggest ways for them to reinforce the school reading program at home.

10. Volunteer to coordinate National Library Week or Children's Book Week with special programs in your school. One school made a large bulletin board with pictures and letters from all of the faculty members telling what books had made the most difference in their lives. Find authors who live in your community who are willing to talk to students

about writing; correspond with authors and publish their letters; or arrange a conference call with a famous author. Invite community leaders and business people to read their favorite stories aloud to classes.

11. Persuade a local business to award young readers with gift certificates to encourage recreational reading. Pizza Hut has had great success with its "Book-It" program which awards certificates for pan pizzas when students reach goals they have set for themselves. Get the community involved.

12. Volunteer to help your child's teacher coordinate a special reading program. Use PTA or school funds to purchase read-aloud tapes and books along with inexpensive tape recorders. Students can check out the tapes and books to take home.

13. Organize a Battle of the Books program for your intermediate students. A reading list of about forty books is selected. Questions are written about each book. Students form teams and then compete by answering questions from the books. This contest is an excellent way to stimulate reading and encourage academic competition.

14. Volunteer to form a parent-teacher committee to involve more parents in the community in the reading achievement of their students.

15. Organize a program in which faculty and administration will report to parents on the academic performance of students in the area of reading.

16. Lead a campaign to establish a library in your school if you don't already have one.

17. Run for the school board and become involved in policy making decisions regarding curriculum. If you're concerned about what is happening in your schools, there is no better place to have an impact.

8

How To Help Your Problem Reader

Saul, a delightful little first grader, had been in three different schools during the year. He entered our school just as the year was coming to a close. Saul didn't know his alphabet, couldn't associate any of the letters with their corresponding sounds, and didn't enjoy hearing the teacher read stories aloud.

Mrs. Karr, the first grade teacher, felt Saul would greatly benefit by repeating first grade. His father was devastated. "I flunked second grade," he said, with tears in his eyes. "I want better for my little boy. Just let me teach him over the summer. I know I can catch him up if you'll give me the chance."

Of course we gave him a chance. Every student and parent deserve the chance to try again. And every teacher and principal should have the belief that all students can learn. If your child has experienced failure and discouragement along the way, she can be helped.

However, as I told Saul's father, your efforts to help your child will take time, patience, understanding, and some professional assistance. With each passing school year of failure and defeat, the layers of discouragement and lack of self-worth make the job more difficult.

Perhaps you identify with Saul's father and have even endured similar parent-teacher conferences. Perhaps your child is a "problem reader." Is he in the "low" reading group? Does he score more than a year below grade level on the standardized tests that are given in school? Does he have difficulty reading and understanding science and history assignments? Does he groan with dread when the teacher assigns a book report? If you answered yes to any of the questions, you are probably living with a "problem reader."

Some parents think that their children have reading problems if they don't enjoy reading or spend time reading recreationally. However, my definition of a child with a reading problem is one whose lack of reading skills keeps him from doing average to above average work in school. A child who cannot gain meaning from the printed word on a par with others at his grade level has a reading problem.

WHY MIGHT MY CHILD HAVE A READING PROBLEM AND *WHAT* CAN BE DONE TO SOLVE THE PROBLEM?

This chapter presents a three-part plan to help solve your child's reading problem. First we'll look at READING RESTRICTORS, specific areas of a child's life and experience that may be interfering with his ability to read well.

Second, we'll gather a READING SAMPLE. We'll find out if your child has specific problems with comprehension, word pronunciation, or fluency and speed.

Finally, we'll look at a READING PLAN for action that will give you suggestions for helping your child immediately.

READING RESTRICTORS

Figuring out why your child is having a reading problem may be a little like solving a mystery. You will need to be a detective to see if any of these "reading restrictors" is having a negative impact on your child's learning. Resources to help you both in and out of the school system are given for each Reading Restrictor.

Health

Children must be able both to see and hear to learn to read. Problems in either area may severely impact reading ability. In ruling out possible causes of learning problems, start here.

Other health problems such as severe allergies or infections which cause a child to miss a great deal of school can impact learning. Regular attendance is very important, especially during instruction in beginning reading. Many children who do poorly in school have simply missed large chunks of instruction and do not have a good foundation on which to base new learnings. Had they been regular attenders, their problems would be far fewer.

In-School Resources: classroom teacher, school nurse.

Out-Of-School Resources: pediatrician, eye doctor, hearing specialist.

School

How can school be a reading restrictor? Unfortunately, in the hands of a poor teacher, even the most dedicated student can have learning problems. Talk with your child regularly about what is happening at school. Look over her papers, go to all scheduled parent conferences, and become an educated consumer of your school system, whether it be Christian or public. (Chapter six gives you ways to help improve your school's reading program.)

In-School Resources: classroom teacher, remedial reading teacher, learning disability resource teacher, principal.

Out-Of-School Resources: parent-teacher organization, commercial reading clinics and tutors.

Mobility

Children who move frequently may miss out on important skills. Make sure when you move that all records are transferred and that you are aware of the reading levels and abilities of your children. Monitor their placement, particularly in reading, as they enter a new school.

In-School Resources: classroom teacher, principal.

Out-Of-School Resources: commercial reading clinics or tutors.

Home

Are there emotional factors in your family that cause your child to lie awake at night and worry? Is school attendance and achievement a low priority in your family? Or are you putting so much pressure on your child that he is responding with nervousness and failure? Do you neglect reading aloud with your children?

Affixing blame is not nearly as important as solving the problem. However, if there are home patterns that should be changed, neglecting to address them will only cause the problem to grow worse.

In-School Resources: classroom teacher, principal, school social worker

Out-Of-School Resources: family counselor or psychologist, Sunday school teacher, pastor, books, audio and video tapes, workshops/programs on parenting.

Learning Ability

The child who appears to have average or above-average intelligence but still has problems learning to read may well have a learning disability. The learning disabled child may have a short attention span, problems organizing himself and his homework, difficulty remembering spelling words, and problems controlling his behavior. Public schools are required by law to evaluate and offer services to children who have diagnosed learning disabilities. Search out help.

In-School Resources: classroom teacher, principal, school psychologist, special education teacher.

Out-Of-School Resources: pediatrician, pediatric neurologist, psychologist.

Language Development

If your child was slow to develop speaking skills and even now has problems expressing herself, she may have speech and language problems that are inhibiting reading achievement. Children need lots of language input from adults to learn sentence structure, vocabulary, and grammar. This learning provides the base on which a child learns to read.

In-School Resources: classroom teacher, speech and language pathologist, school psychologist, principal.

Out-Of-School Resources: speech and hearing clinics, hearing specialist.

Social and Emotional Development

This last restrictor of reading achievement is most often seen in older children and adolescents. Problems that were evident in preschool and early elementary years may have been allowed to go untended. Layers of failure and discouragement often result in students with poor attitudes or severe discipline problems. Most adolescents would rather be thought of as "smart alecky" or "troublesome" than "dumb." Their feelings of self-defeat come out in anti-social ways, and we often fail to connect them with the obvious academic problems.

In-School Resources: classroom teacher, principal, school social worker, counselor, psychologist.

Out-Of-School Resources: youth pastor, pastor, family counselor or psychologist, learning/motivation clinics, psychiatrist, psychiatric social worker.

READING SAMPLE

The next step in helping to solve your child's reading problem is to obtain a reading sample. You will need to spend three sessions with your child, each twenty to thirty minutes, listening to your child read aloud. If your child attends school and has a basal reading text, get permission from the teacher to use the text for three evenings. Explain that you want to hear your child read aloud. If your child is older, use a science, social studies, or literature textbook.

During these read-aloud sessions, avoid pressuring or blaming your child. You are simply gathering information that will help you make decisions about how best to improve your child's reading ability. Follow these simple steps:

1. Set aside three twenty-to-thirty-minute blocks of time to read with your child.

2. Use your child's current reading book or other textbook if appropriate and choose a story or selection that he has not yet read and discussed in school.

3. Have your child read the selection aloud.

4. Keep track of errors in pronunciation and omission of words and phrases. Five or more errors in a 100-word sample indicate there may be *accuracy* problems in her reading.

5. Ask your child *ten* questions about the story. They will test *comprehension*. Ask some factual questions: How many apples did Sally buy? Where did she buy them? Ask some inference questions: Why do you think Sally bought ten apples? Ask some sequence questions: Where did Sally go first after school? Where did she go next?

If your child answered three or more questions wrong, he may have *comprehension* problems.

6. Note your child's *reading rate*. Does he read at a conversational rate, somewhat slowly, or very slowly?

Identify Problem Areas:
As a result of the reading sample, you should have some idea of where your child's reading problems lie.

☐ Decoding: ability to decipher and pronounce new words.

☐ Vocabulary: ability to figure out the meaning of new words.

☐ Comprehension/factual: ability to answer questions about what has happened in this story.

☐ Comprehension/inferential: ability to "read between the lines" and draw conclusions about the story.

☐ Comprehension/sequencing: ability to place events in their proper sequence in the story.

☐ Reading rate: ability to read at an appropriate rate so that fluency is maintained.

Knowing where your child has specific problems will enable you to focus on certain skills when you spend time reading aloud with your child.

First you thought about possible reasons *why* your child might have reading problems. Next you closely examined your child's reading to determine *what* specific problems existed. Now you are ready to take some action that may begin to solve the problem. The Action Plan for Improving Reading Skills will give you definite suggestions for *how* to do this.

ACTION PLAN FOR IMPROVING READING SKILLS

Part I: Work through each of the following questions in order.

1. Were there any indications when your child was an infant, toddler, or preschooler that a learning disability might exist?

☐ extremely short attention span
☐ hyperactivity
☐ memory problems
☐ poor motor coordination
☐ delays in language development

No: Go on to question 2.

Yes: Talk with school personnel about special testing for learning disabilities. In addition, you may wish to consult a pediatric neurologist to determine if physiological problems are interfering with learning.

2. Did you read aloud to your child on a regular basis throughout his early years?

No: Begin reading aloud with your child immediately. Junior high or high school students who are having difficulty with history, science, or literature courses can profit from reading aloud with their parents and discussing questions with them.

Yes: Go on to question 3.

3. Did your child have trouble learning his alphabet and letter sounds because you moved or he was absent a great deal during kindergarten or first grade?

No: Go on to question 4.

Yes: Your child may have missed out on some important learning. Either through the school or a reading clinic, have your child tested on beginning phonics to see whether any "chunks" of learning are missing. If you find this to be the case, find a tutor or reading clinic that will teach your child how to sound out and "attack" new words.

4. Did your child ever see a special reading teacher during his early school career?

No: Go on to question 5.

Yes: If possible arrange to meet with that teacher or review the records to determine what methods were used during that time. The teacher who worked with your child might be a valuable resource in sharing information about your child's learning style and which methods of teaching were most effective. Or you might determine that the methods and approach used in the program did not meet your child's needs and a different approach is needed for your child to experience success.

5. Does your child hate to read?

No: Go on to question 6.

Yes: Set aside some time to talk with your child about his perceptions of reading. When did he begin to feel like a failure? What teachers helped him most? Slow readers have a different perception of reading than proficient readers. Problem readers think reading is getting the words right, sounding the words out, or doing schoolwork. Good readers think reading is pleasurable, a way to find out information, and a socially acceptable way to spend time.

6. In your zeal to improve your child's reading do you make fun of her attempts to read "easy" material and/or continually press for the reading of more difficult and challenging books?

No: Go on to question 7.

Yes: Examine whether you are hindering your child's comprehension more than helping. Children need time, encouragement, and constant exposure to language. They need to reread stories and passages several times until they can read them fluently. They need to read selections that are easy and fun. All of this needs to be done in an atmosphere of acceptance and support.

7. Have you heard yourself or your child's teacher say: "He's really a bright kid. Too bad he's not working up to his potential."

No: Go on to question 8.

Yes: Think about having your child evaluated professionally for a possible learning disability. Learning disabled children have average or above average ability but are unable to translate that ability into success in school. Understanding the reasons for the problem and building on your child's learning strengths will frequently change a pattern of failure. Along with getting help for the academic problems comes the need for counseling and help for the student emotionally and psychologically.

8. Have you tried in many ways over the years to help your child with reading, but become frustrated with your lack of success?

No: Go on to question 9.

Yes: Examine how you have been trying to help. The method we used to gain information about your child's reading strengths and weaknesses has been used very effectively with all kinds of students to improve reading comprehension. If you use the method for thirty minutes per day with your child, you will immediately begin to see an improvement. A grandparent, baby-sitter, or a hired high school student can also be very effective as a tutor.

The secret is consistency, calmness, and expectations. Consistency means spending thirty minutes per day without fail. Calmness means that when your child makes a mistake or doesn't know an answer, you don't blame or raise your voice. Expectations means that you expect your child to achieve a certain level in comprehension, accuracy, and reading rate before you go on to another story. If a child needs to reread a story three or four times to achieve that level, you will do so together in a calm way. Perhaps we need to look at reading more like playing the piano. Practicing the same piece several times is the only way to get it absolutely right. Take the same approach with reading.

9. Does your child's teacher have high expectations for his reading performance?

No: Talk with your child's teacher and observe in the classroom. Teachers frequently expect less from students in low reading groups. They ask fewer questions of these students and the questions they do ask are often easier. Reading materials used for low reading groups are frequently boring and contain many skill pages that offer little opportunity for truly practicing reading.

Students perceived by teachers as slower learners are frequently given less time to think about answering a question before the teacher moves on to another student. Communicate your expectations to the teacher that your child will do well in reading and your willingness to help the teacher in any way. Offer to help your child with reading assignments at home.

Yes: Support, encourage, and pray for that teacher as she works with your child.

Part II: Proceed to implement your own plan of action using the following guidelines.

• If you have determined that any of the reading restrictors are keeping your child from doing his best, consult resources both in and out of school to determine what can be done.

• Make a plan for your child that includes special help at school, outside counseling or tutoring as appropriate, and a program of special help at home.

• Read aloud to your child every day for at least fifteen minutes no matter what his age. If your child has book reports or literature classes, read aloud some of these assignments with her.

• Incorporate as many of the following activities into your family life as possible:

Read the Bible aloud each night at the dinner table if you do not already do so. This activity will result in spiritual as well as academic benefits. Have different family members take turns with the reading. (See chapter five for recommended read-aloud Bibles and Bible storybooks.)

Visit the children's library and browse through the periodical section. Try to find a magazine that will interest your child and purchase a subscription.

Play games that involve reading. Scrabble, Boggle, Password, Probe, and Spill and Spell build vocabulary and encourage discussion about words and their meanings.

If your child watches TV, steer him to programs that have related book titles.

Take your child shopping in a bookstore and allow him to buy several titles that interest him.

Encourage your child to buy paperback books from the school book fair or paperback book clubs.

Visit the library at church. Check out a variety of titles

until you find a series that appeals to your child. Purchase copies of the series so that favorites can be reread.

Set aside a fifteen minute period each evening when everyone in the family reads silently together in the same room.

Our children are God's most precious gifts to us. As you begin to work with your child, pray that He will guide and direct each step of your plan. He alone can give you the courage, guidance, and wisdom to effect change in your child's life.

9

How *Not* To Raise A Reader

Two of the most marvelous gadgets that technology has given us are the fast-forward and pause buttons on the video recorder. We can fast-forward through commercials or slow-moving parts of the plot. Conversely, we can pause on a particular frame and freeze it while we study some specific detail in the picture.

Let's fast forward to the future and examine some family scenes that are likely to occur as your children grow older, move through the various stages of reading, and begin to assert their individuality and personalities through their reading. We'll pause at each scene and examine it to help you keep from making some major mistakes as you raise a reader.

RULE NUMBER ONE: DON'T USE READING ALOUD TO RAISE A SUPERKID.

From the minute we marry, anxious, prospective grandparents are breathing over our shoulders wondering if we're expecting. Once the long-awaited child arrives, there are weekly phone calls to find out if young junior is smiling, crawling, talking, walking, and even reading.

We are under tremendous pressures as parents to raise "superkids." In my suburban area there are dozens of courses and programs in which to enroll very small children. Parents 157 are willing, it seems, to pay for any program that will give their child the "edge." Many early childhood researchers warn against exposing young children to too much formal education. They feel, and I agree, that very young children do not learn in the structured and programmed ways that are appropriate for older learners.

Reading aloud to your child should not be a formal, structured program. You are not teaching him to read. You are spending time with your child reading to him. He will learn in his own way and in his own time. You have no way of knowing how much learning is going on.

My recent experience with growing grass from seed has some parallel features. I purchased the seed. I read the directions. I scattered the seed along with fertilizer and I began to water. The box said to keep the seed wet and emphasized the importance of daily watering. A couple of days, I didn't feel like watering. I couldn't see anything happening. But I did it anyhow. The habit was ingrained.

Even after the seed was supposed to have germinated and I still didn't see results, I watered. Just when I was beginning to think my efforts were for naught, I glimpsed a few green shoots. I had to look closely. Now I was more motivated to water. But still I doubted the worth of my efforts. "It's never going to get really green and full like the picture on the box," I lamented to my husband.

"Just keep watering," he said. "I'll take the next few days if you're getting weary of it." Each day, more green shoots poked through the soil. At a distance, there was a light covering of green fuzz. My efforts were beginning to pay off. I couldn't stop watering, however. The new, green shoots needed constant attention. They needed more fertilizer, even a little weed killer, as they grew stronger.

Those green shoots are like your child's reading ability. The printed word is the seed and your reading aloud is the watering. During much of the time you are reading aloud, you will never know what is being learned. But you must have faith that if you water (read) during this germination period, the seed (your child's reading ability) will grow and flourish.

RULE NUMBER TWO: LET YOUR CHILD MAKE CHOICES ABOUT *WHAT* TO READ.

You're bone weary. The day has been filled with a number of minor irritants—a cranky child who is teething, a broken washing machine, a misunderstanding with a co-worker. You finally get the kids ready for bed and look forward with longing to a few minutes of quiet before tackling the dinner dishes. The children remind you with glee that you've forgotten their bedtime story.

You want to read a new book you've just checked out of the library. Preferably something short and snappy with lots of pictures. The children want to hear *Bread and Jam for Frances.* "But," you protest, "we've read that one before." You've read the book so often that your mouth ceases to water any more at the delightful descriptions of the meals Frances' mother fixes to lure her away from eating bread and jam.

Impatient and irritable you raise your voice just above its normal tone and assert your parental rights. "We're not reading that book again. We've read it before!" You lose the argument and for very good reasons.

When our first child was born after five years of being a two-career couple, my husband didn't turn into superdad overnight. He was a bit reluctant to become involved with the more mundane tasks like diapers and meals. Any time I left home for more than an hour, he needed several pages of instructions regarding what to do next.

Then one Sunday night I was having severe abdominal pains and drove myself to the local hospital. My husband was more than a little upset that I was leaving him with a spunky three year old and a just-learning-to-walk one year old and taking the only car in the family along with me.

"You'll be OK," I told him. "If anybody wakes up, feed

them a peanut butter and jelly sandwich and read them a story."

"What kind of story?" he quizzed me.

"They have their favorites. Just read the same one over and over again."

"I'll go crazy," my husband responded.

"I know!" I smiled. "But you'll be OK. I probably won't be gone too long." I was at the hospital for a week. My nearly ruptured appendix was gangrenous.

That was the week that my husband became a real father. Not only did he discover how much work is involved in parenting small children, he got hooked on reading books aloud to the kids. "I don't think I can stand to read *Small Pig* one more time," he moaned in one of our many hospital to home phone conversations. "Why do they have to hear the same stories so many times?"

I didn't have the time to explain to him then that children have an insatiable need to hear the same stories, poems, and rhymes over and over again. I think we were interrupted by the diaper delivery man arriving with reinforcements.

Our adult brains can tolerate perhaps a dozen readings of *George and Martha* before the plot becomes fairly predictable. Unless you understand the importance that repetition plays in the development of the child, you will be tempted to utter those words: "We've read that book before."

Remember: you are reading the book from the perspective of an adult. Each time you read the book aloud to your child, a new word may become part of her vocabulary, a new insight about a relationship or small detail of the story will become clear, or some part of an illustration will suddenly be noticed for the first time.

And then there is the sheer joy of hearing the language used in all of the wonderful ways that authors and poets have put it together. Do you tire of hearing the pastor read the 23rd Psalm, particularly when you are in need of solace or comfort? Do you stand up in church on Sunday when the

Doxology is sung to shout—"We've sung that one before."
Then, don't be guilty of deciding for your child that he can't
hear *Bread and Jam for Frances* just one more time.

At the same time, your choice of read-alouds becomes
important. You want your child's range of choices to be from a
group that you feel is acceptable. You get to decide for the
very small child what books will be read aloud. Read them
yourself ahead of time. Choose from among the many suggestions provided in earlier chapters. Choose from the marvelous selections at public libraries, Christian and secular
bookstores, or your church library. Ask yourself: "Is this a
story that I'll enjoy reading over and over?"

We frequently parent our toddlers like teenagers. We
allow them to set their own limits and make too many decisions for themselves. Conversely, we parent teenagers like
toddlers. We dictate, set limits, and try to make their choices.
My point is simply this—you choose, from among thousands
available, those books that you feel are the very best. Then
give your child the opportunity to decide which of those many
he would like to hear over and over—the books that will become a part of his childhood memories.

Boys and girls in the preschool and early elementary
years soon begin to make more of their own choices from the
library shelves. They will often bring books home from their
school libraries for you to read aloud. They may sometimes
choose books that aren't well written or have a point of view
with which you disagree. At this point you can become the
literary critic and point out why you personally do not care
for the book.

Your children respect your judgment and at this age will
be willing listeners to your ideas and opinions. Now is the
time to begin subtly shaping their choices and explaining the
reasons why certain books or stories are not worthy of their
consideration. This is also the time to begin exploring non-
fiction, magazines, and encyclopedias.

As children grow older and begin to read more independently, the area of choice can become a battleground. You may think that what your child is reading is not appropriate. You may feel your child is choosing material that is too easy or too repetitious. Children often get in reading ruts with series like Nancy Drew, the Hardy Boys, or the Choose Your Own Adventure series. We think our children are wasting time. We think they should realize after reading the first two in a series that the plots are all alike, that the characters are trite, that they are reading the same story seven different ways.

I'm not certain how many Grace Livingston Hill novels I borrowed from the church library before I realized that I knew the stories better than Grace did. The point is, let your child make the choice. Left to explore various styles and types of writing, the child will soon become bored and move on to other more challenging choices.

Your child may choose reading materials that seem inappropriate. Hence the battlecry: "You can't read that. That's trash."

Here the issue of having faith in your child's ability to choose and make judgments about what is well written and worthy of acceptance and what is poorly written and worthy of rejection comes into play. Discuss with your child why you like or dislike certain authors or styles of writing. Then permit your child to choose for himself based on the foundation you've laid in the early years. Early exposure to good writing and Christian values will allow your young person to make his own decisions wisely as he reaches maturity. The exciting part is seeing him make choices on his own that parallel the ones you would have made for him.

RULE NUMBER THREE: LET YOUR CHILD MAKE CHOICES ABOUT *WHEN* TO READ

Matt hadn't always been the most enthusiastic student. For most of his school years he had barely scraped by. Maybe the fact that his family moved every year or two just ahead of the rent collector gave him little incentive to try in school. Just as soon as he tried to fit in or make a friend, he overhead conversations late at night about packing up and moving on. But his new fifth-grade teacher made school different. She had a fantastic way of making him want to read books. Matt really began to look forward to going to school. Miss Lindvall set aside time every day for all the kids in the class to read silently, and she read aloud every day, too.

The book she was reading now was called *Where the Red Fern Grows,* and Matt had been able to check out a copy from the public library. There were parts in it that almost made him want to cry they were so sad. He was reading right along with the teacher. The only problem was at home. Every time he sat down to reread some of the good parts, his mother yelled at him. "Why don't you go outside and play? You're going to get sick if you stay inside and read all the time."

Maybe you grew up in a household like Matt's—or maybe one like mine. Whenever I sat down with a book, someone was right there thinking up something else for me to do. I grew up in a Dutch household where there were strict schedules about when certain tasks would be performed. Washing of clothes always occurred on Mondays. Tuesday was reserved for ironing. On Wednesday one half of the house was cleaned and on Thursday the remaining half was thoroughly scrubbed down. Friday was grocery shopping and baking day. Saturday was spent getting ready for Sunday— polishing shoes, peeling potatoes and cleaning vegetables for Sunday dinner. But on Sunday, after Sunday school, the morning service, and a generous dinner, the afternoon was all mine. Thank goodness for Sundays!

The hours until we reassembled as a family to attend the evening service were free. Since we never engaged in any physical activity on Sundays, swimming and playing ball were out. Even sewing or doing homework stretched the strict Dutch interpretation of how the Lord's Day should be spent. Reading, however, was acceptable and it was the one time of the week when Mother didn't mind if we "did nothing."

I would find a corner in the house or yard and curl up. In the summertime, I'd go out into the apple orchard and find a cozy spot all by myself. My reading choices came from the bookmobile that serviced our rural area once a week. I loved the Laura Ingalls Wilder stories and always tried to get at least one in my weekly allotment. But mysteries were my real favorites. Sunday afternoons flew by, and I was always reluctant to put my books away and go in for supper.

If you raise a reader, you must be prepared that your reader will so enjoy spending time with a book that she will want to read when you think she should be doing something else, like sleeping or cleaning her room. Any issue can become a power struggle between parent and child. If you didn't like to read as a child, you may be tempted to think your child is trying to avoid doing what you want her to do. What you should remember is that once you've raised a reader, you must be prepared for the fact that some books need to be finished in one sitting.

Sometimes you just can't turn out the light until you've finished a chapter. Please be understanding, parents, and let your reader read when she wants to, within pre-established limits. A better technique is to set a deadline: Your room must be cleaned by tomorrow night before bedtime. Your light must be out after you read three more chapters.

Reading is a valid use of time for a child. We will never know what ideas, knowledge, understanding, or desires are kindled in the mind of a child through a book. Books inspire careers, change our thinking, even change the course of history.

RULE NUMBER FOUR: LET YOUR CHILD MAKE CHOICES ABOUT *HOW MUCH TO READ.*

My son Patrick and I were in the children's department

of the local public library. A father and daughter (she was about four or five) were selecting picture books together. I was eavesdropping as I frequently do on conversations between parents and children. She had an armload of books and proudly brought them to her father. He turned to her and said in a sharp voice, "Put all those books back. You can only take three." The rule was parent imposed. Our library very wisely places no limit on the number of books that can be checked out.

My son looked at me and smiled. We were both remembering the quantities of books that we had checked out of the library when he was the little girl's age. We took shopping bags and filled them to overflowing. We took as many books as we could carry at one time and sometimes came back for a second load. There was always just one more that we needed to have. I think I had the fear that we might run out in the middle of a snowstorm or on a Sunday when the library was closed. For the parent who so frequently has to limit the appetites of children, the public library is a delightful place to be. Rarely do we need to say no.

RULE NUMBER FIVE: DON'T USE READING AS A FORM OF PUNISHMENT.

Let's put the video recorder on pause and take a look at one last family scene. Maybe this one has happened in your household.

Sandy wasn't doing particularly well in school. Her teacher didn't seem to understand the real reason she went to school—to be with her friends. Mrs. Greider wasn't terribly sympathetic about Sandy's late homework assignments or the reading test she failed because she was so upset about her fight with Amy. But if Sandy's teacher wasn't sympathetic, her parents were downright hostile about her failing grade in reading. They decided that if Sandy wasn't going to work in school, she could certainly work at home.

Every night right after school she would sit at the kitchen table and READ for one hour. Her father decided reading the Bible would be the ideal activity for a child who wasn't fulfilling school responsibilities. Sandy had always enjoyed reading for pleasure. She also enjoyed the times after dinner when her father read from the Scriptures. But the enforced reading of God's Word, after she had put in a full day at school, was pure torture. It wasn't long before reading was no longer any fun. Reading had turned into a family battle.

Sandy's problems with school should certainly not have been ignored. However, reading as punishment did not improve reading achievement, much less cultivate a love of reading or of God's Word.

The challenge to us as parents comes in applying these rules to the lives of our children. You too can raise a reader!

10

Every Child
Can Be
A Reader

If you read a book as I often do, then this chapter might be the first place you've turned. In that case, you have an opportunity to preview the key themes of this book. To those readers who have read this book in a more traditional way, I hope the following will serve to reinforce what you've been reading and thinking about along the way.

• Reading is one of the most important skills your child will need to acquire in life.

• Reading is an especially important part of the Christian life since we must be able to read God's Word in order to nourish our faith.

• The read-aloud experience is one of the most important activities that can develop good readers.

• All Christian parents have the responsibility to read aloud to their children on a regular basis.

• Although reading aloud to children should begin when they are infants and continue indefinitely, you can begin when your children are older.

• The read-aloud experience can be a delightful one, because there are hundreds of wonderful books to choose from, both Christian and secular.

• You can entice even the most reluctant reader by providing an ample supply of easy-to-read books with predictable plots and easy vocabulary.

• Christian parents have a responsibility to evaluate and become involved in their child's school. Don't assume that your school can teach reading without your help!

• There is help if your child is a problem reader, but you will have to make a commitment of time and energy to become involved.

• In all of our endeavors to raise children—especially children who can read, we need the guidance and direction of God.

If you're a new parent, I envy your experiences in the next few years. My early parenting days are among my most treasured memories. Begin reading aloud immediately.

If you're the parent of a reluctant reader, begin to think about what you can do to support and help your child to be a better reader. But most importantly, read aloud.

If you're the parent of children who enjoy reading, begin now to read God's Word aloud at your dinner table on a regular basis. Share the responsibility among all family members.

If you're a teacher, grandparent, or spend time with children in any other capacity, begin now to plan how you can add the read-aloud experience to the time you share with these children.

Having raised two readers of my own, I'm convinced that the principles set forth in this book will work for you. I also know that you and your children will be blessed and enriched as you spend time reading aloud together.

Notes

Chapter One

[1]Albert J. Harris and Edward R. Sipay, *Effective Teaching of Reading,* New York: McKay, 1971. p. 13.

[2]Burton J. White, *The First Three Years of Life,* Englewood Cliffs, New Jersey: Prentice Hall; 1975. p. 111.

[3]Margaret Clark, *Young Fluent Readers,* London: Heinemann, 1976. Dolores Durkin, "Children Who Learned to Read at Home," *Elementary School Journal,* Vol. 62 (October, 1961). Dolores Durkin, "An Earlier Start in Reading?" *Elementary School Journal,* Vol. 63 (December, 1962). Dolores Durkin, "Children Who Read Before Grade 1: A Second Study," *Elementary School Journal,* Vol. 64 (December, 1963). Dolores Durkin, *Children Who Read Early,* New York: Teachers College Press, 1966. William H. Teale, "Positive Environment for Learning to Read: What Studies of Early Readers Tell Us," *Language Arts,* Vol. 55 (November December, 1978).

[4]White, op. cit.

Chapter Two

[1]Joan Beck, *How to Raise a Brighter Child,* New York: Trident Press, 1967.

[2]Polly Berrien Berends, *Whole Child, Whole Parent,* New York: Harpers Magazine Press, 1975. Dorothy Butler, *Babies Need Books,* New York: Atheneum, 1982. Bernice Cullinan, *Literature and the Child,* New York: Harcourt Brace Jovanovich, 1981. Kate Hall McMullan, *How to Choose Good Books for Kids,* Reading, Massachusetts: Addison-Wesley Publishing Co., 1984. Nancy L. Nehmer, *A Parent's Guide to Christian Books for Children,* Wheaton, Illinois: Tyndale, 1984. Jim Trelease, *The Read-Aloud Handbook,* New York: Penguin, 1985.

[3]White, op. cit., pp. 29-30.

Bibliography

Ames, Louise Bates, and Frances L. Ilg. *Your Five Year Old*. New York: Delacorte, 1979.

Ames, Louise Bates, and Frances L. Ilg. *Your Four Year Old*. New York: Delacorte, 1976.

Ames, Louise Bates, and Frances L. Ilg. *Your Six Year Old*. New York: Delacorte, 1979.

Beck, Joan. *How to Raise a Brighter Child*. New York: Trident, 1967.

Berends, Polly Berrien. *Whole Child, Whole Parent*. New York: Harpers Magazine Press, 1975.

Butler, Dorothy. *Babies Need Books*. New York: Atheneum, 1982.

Butler, Dorothy and Marie Clay. *Reading Begins at Home*. Exeter, New Hampshire: Heinemann Educational Books, 1979.

Cascardi, Andrea E. *Good Books to Grow On*. New York: Warner Books, 1985.

Chomsky, Carol. "Stages in Language Development and Reading Exposure." *Harvard Educational Review*, Vol. 42, 1971, pp. 1–33.

Clark, Margaret M. *Young Fluent Readers*. London: Heinemann, 1976.

Copperman, Paul. *Taking Books to Heart: How to Develop a Love of Reading in Your Child*. Reading, Massachusetts: Addison-Wesley, 1986.

Cullinan, Bernice. *Literature and the Child*. New York: Harcourt Brace Jovanovich, 1981.

Doman, Glenn. *How to Teach Your Baby to Read*. New York: Random House, 1963.

Durkin, Dolores, "Children Who Learned to Read at Home." *Elementary School Journal*. Vol. 62, Oct., 1961.

Durkin, Dolores. "An Earlier Start in Reading?" *Elementary School Journal*, Vol. 63, Dec., 1962.

Durkin, Dolores. "Children Who Read Before Grade 1: A Second Study." *Elementary School Journal*, Vol. 64, Dec., 1963.

Durkin, Dolores. *Children Who Read Early*. New York: Teachers College Press, 1966.

Elkind, David. *The Hurried Child*. Reading, Massachusetts: Addison-Wesley, 1981.

Elkind, David. *The Miseducation of Children: Superkids at Risk*. New York: Knopf, 1986.

Ervin, Jane. *Your Child Can Read and You Can Help*. New York: Doubleday, 1979.

Forgan, Harry W. *Help Your Child Learn to Read*. Toronto: Pagurian Press Ltd., 1975.

Gesell, Arnold L., Frances L. Ilg, and Louise Bates Ames. *The Child From Five to Ten*. New York: Harper & Row, 1946.

Harris, Albert J. & Edward R. Sipay. *Effective Teaching of Reading*. New York: McKay, 1971.

Hunt, Gladys. *Honey For a Child's Heart*. Grand Rapids, Michigan: Zondervan, 1969.

Kimmel, Margaret Mary and Elizabeth Segel. *For Reading Out Loud: A Guide to Sharing Books with Children*. New York: 1983.

Lamme, Linda with Vivian Cox, Janet Matanzo and Miken Olson. *Raising Readers: A Guide to Sharing Literature with Young Children*. New York: Walker & Co., 1980.

McMullan, Kate Hall. *How to Choose Good Books for Kids*. Reading, Massachusetts: Addison-Wesley, 1984.

Nehmer, Nancy L. *A Parent's Guide to Christian Books for Children*. Wheaton, Illinois: Tyndale, 1984.

Sabine, Gordon and Patricia. *Books That Made the Difference*. Hamden, Connecticut: Shoe String Press, 1983.

Smith, Frank. *Understanding Reading*. New York: Holt, Rinehart & Winston, 1971.

Teale, William H. "Positive Environment for Learning To Read: What Studies of Early Readers Tell Us." *Language Arts* Vol. 55, Nov/Dec., 1978, pp. 922–32.

Trelease, Jim. *The Read-Aloud Handbook*. New York: Penguin, 1979.

White, Burton J. *The First Three Years of Life*. Englewood Cliffs, New Jersey: Prentice Hall, 1975.

White, Dorothy. *Books Before Five*. Portsmouth, New Hampshire: Heinemann Educational Books, 1984.

Yolen, Jane. *Touch Magic*. New York: Philomel, 1981.

Index

AUTHOR/*ILLUSTRATOR*

*All italicized names denote illustrator.